Parenting Abroad

Ngaire Jehle-Caitcheon

Parenting Abroad

Ngaire
Jehle-Caitcheon

ALETHEIA
Publications

Jehle-Caitcheon, Ngaire
Parenting Abroad

Library of Congress Control Number: 2002113017
ISBN: 1-929129-03-3

Cover design: Bart Solenthaler
Interior design and composition: Guy J. Smith

Aletheia Publications, Inc.
46 Bell Hollow Rd.
Putnam Valley, NY 10579

Printed in Canada

10 9 8 7 6 5 4 3 2 1

Contents

Acknowledgments

I would like to thank the hundreds of parents and children and scores of teachers and psychologists whose thoughts and sentiments are echoed in this book. My particular thanks go to Billie Anne Lopez and Vinal Binner, whose guidance and support have kept the writing process going, and my husband, whose eye for detail never failed.

My greatest debt is owed to Urs, Senta, and Nick, who taught me that families *can* survive and thrive abroad even in the face of crises. And our family owes a debt we can never repay to the people who supported us through these crises, including those who literally saved our lives. Those who did not survive live on in our hearts.

Chapter 1
The Overseas Assignment

To go or not to go,
To stay or not to stay,
Those are the questions.

Paul, moving from Milan to Dar es Salam and on to Tokyo, goes through the same developmental stages as
Christopher, growing up in London, but Paul's environments are radically different and constantly changing.
Because he is still developing, the impact of any one move
will be different. He moved to Dar es Salam as a toddler,
to Tokyo in the fourth grade. Now, at 14, he and his family are preparing to move again. In each place his parents
have had to make a lot of decisions for him, even when
they were not really familiar with the environment.
Where should they send a 4-year-old to kindergarten in
Dar es Salam? Was it safe for their 12-year-old to use the

subway alone in Tokyo? For Paul to weather so many changes, his parents have to provide a lot of support. The problem is that they must cope with the same changes without much support for themselves.

*R*aising children abroad is the same as at home, yet it is completely different. Are you a parent considering an international move, or are you already living abroad? The question of what an international life means for your children is an important one. Should we even take our children to another country? Does it do them any good? Does it do them any harm? And what does it mean for us as parents? What extra challenges do we face? Will we be able to do a good job of bringing up our children in foreign countries?

When our family fled crisis situations in Liberia and then in Zaire, I wondered what we were doing to our children—and what we were doing to ourselves. But these days our children take all sorts of situations in their stride. Grown and almost grown, they have their ups and downs, but they are capable of riding the waves of change. Their knowledge and understanding of others lends them a degree of compassion and empathy that I struggle to emulate. I consider raising them my greatest achievement, and raising them abroad the most interesting thing I have ever done.

Living Abroad With Children

Living abroad with our children has been an adventure within an adventure. Before becoming parents in Switzerland, then moving with our little daughter and infant son to Saudi Arabia, my husband and I had traveled a lot. We had ridden on the tops of buses in Nepal, trekked the jungles of Northern Thailand, feasted on strawberries in Kabul. We thought we knew all about traveling until we became expatriate parents. Then the real adventure began. We were suddenly thrown into closer contact with strangers who petted, smiled at, berated, or filled our young children to the brim with local sweets. We watched with joy as our children interacted with all sorts of people, and with consternation as they adopted ways of doing things that were strange to us. Each situation raised questions about how we should bring them up and what we should teach them, leading us on a parallel journey of discovery of our own cultures and values.

Parenting abroad is no sinecure, even though some of the benefits can make it look that way. Having household help, for instance, gets the dishes done and lets us go off to yoga class, but it does not get the real parenting job done. We still have to comfort the child who has had to leave pets behind or can't find friends at a new school. Parenting in a country where you can't speak the language and don't know the way to the nearest hospital, or even how to do the shopping, is hardly easy. And just when we most need extra support, we find ourselves alone, far from our usual support systems.

At the same time, good parenting becomes doubly important. Children moving abroad face many challenges, from school and language changes to identity issues. The impact of living abroad is much greater on children. While for us, going to Johannesburg or Paris is an adventure, a career opportunity, an extended vacation, or just something to get through, for our children it is part of the serious business of growing up. While we have fully developed personalities and cultural identities, our children's experiences abroad become part of their developing personalities. Their contact with host cultures is often more intense than ours. Young children make friends faster and people interact more with children. They will smile at a small child, get angry with a teenager, and start a conversation with a youngster in a shop, even when they hesitate to initiate contact with foreign adults.

Expatriate Children

What are expatriate children like? If you observe a group of students at an international school, they look like children the world over. And if you listen in, they'll be discussing the same topics as any other group of children: friends, grades, teachers or whom they like or don't like. They are reassuringly the same as children everywhere, but at the same time they are different. Their daily lives are different from those of their counterparts at home, and their conversations often contain references to exchange rates, qualifier miles, a climb up Mount Kilimanjaro, or the political situation in any one of many countries. In most groups of children you'll also hear a collage of languages.

Expatriate children experience a mixture of privilege and challenge. They have many opportunities, but they live in an environment that is challenging for most adults, let alone for developing youngsters. How well they manage depends to some extent on the balance of opportunity and challenge, but even more on the support they receive. Help and encouragement allow them to take advantage of the good things about living abroad and to cope with the challenges. None of the advantages of living abroad can be taken for granted, just as none of the disadvantages is inevitable.

Expatriate children have the opportunity to learn many skills. Most become more adaptable and develop techniques for managing new situations. Put experienced, well-balanced expatriate children in a new place, and before the dust settles they are planning how to get around and sizing people up, figuring out who might make a good friend. Because their friends come from all over the world, they learn to accept and communicate with others who are different, even when such communication is difficult. In international schools, with students of so many nationalities, there is inevitably some tension and conflict, and children must learn to deal with this and to acknowledge diverse perspectives. In general, children's understanding and empathy go beyond our own resolutions to respect other people's beliefs. They often take other people's perspectives into account without even thinking about it, a skill that parents who have grown up in one country and culture can find difficult to emulate.

Children also learn tangible skills. Many expatriate children speak more than one language, and their knowledge of the world is large, if eclectic. Unfortunately, these abilities are not always valued back home, and when they return home, many children are upset that these skills are no longer needed or used.

They take the rejection of their abilities as a personal affront. However, these skills also lead to other, more subtle developments. A stimulating environment promotes cognitive growth and contributes to lateral thinking. A wide range of experiences promotes innovative and creative thinking.

Expatriate children have opportunities both in the present and in the future. Many attend private international schools where, with a maximum class size of twenty children, they receive personal attention. The overseas packages offered by many organizations provide most families with a higher disposable income than they could earn at home. Most expatriate children are also able to travel more than their peers. Children benefit from future opportunities as well. The need for employees who can work in a global environment has never been greater, and who better than people who have grown up in this environment to fill that need in business, the diplomatic world, and international organizations.

However, privilege comes at a cost. While expatriate children get to see the world, some feel rootless. Most become adaptable, but they may continue adapting forever, failing to find a balance in relationships or unable to settle. Becoming multicultural or multilingual can come at the price of wondering who they are. For many children, friendships end abruptly when they or their friends leave for home or a new posting. They miss the opportunity to develop lasting friendships, to learn the skills they need to maintain friendships, or to develop the trust needed to form deeper relationships. Some come to believe that no one can understand them. After all, who else has lived the same kind of life? There can be other emotional costs, too. Frequent transitions can have lasting effects on children's perceptions and temperament. Each transition produces a period during which they feel dislocated, negative, and isolated, and when transfer periods are short, children often emerge from this period only to undergo another move.

Children who move frequently can end up with educational "gaps." They invariably repeat something or miss something because of differences among the various schools they

attend. Even international schools vary. They are independent organizations, with different school cultures and syl-
labuses. Schools that are accredited by authorities in a home
country, such as the United States or Germany, may still
vary because they are associated with regional rather than
national bodies. French schools are an exception; they follow a national curriculum both in France and abroad. For
many children, changing schools means changing languages. Although most children can change their educational language, experts estimate that it takes between three
and seven years to bring a foreign language to the same
level as the mother tongue. Learning a new language is a
lengthy process, and other subjects are compromised in
the meantime.

> Heiner was an expatriate child. Today, a very successful busi-
> nessman, he believes that the flexibility he learned abroad
> has helped him adapt to the ever-changing marketplace. Karl,
> overwhelmed by his traveling childhood, hopes never to
> move again. He found even a recent apartment change trau-
> matic. "I hated the new apartment at first. I just wanted to be
> back in my old apartment. I know I'll get used to it in time,
> but I hope that I don't have to change again."

However, children can face challenges rather than succumb to them.
Opportunity and risk in the expatriate context are often two
sides of the same coin. Some children, for instance, are proud
of their ties to more than one country; others feel overwhelmed.
However, the key to rising to challenges rather than being
overwhelmed by them lies in the support received. Few children thrive abroad without supportive parenting.

The Parenting Key

> Kyoko says, "When I used to see Sacho yelling at his friends
> in Spanish and…well just being like them, I didn't feel very
> well. The moment he stepped out the door he was so differ-
> ent. It was almost as if he wasn't my son. My husband didn't
> really understand. He thought it was cute, this little 4-year-

old running around with his Guatemalan friends. I think,
now that I have got used to it, there are things I like. He is
so lively and funny."

*To a large extent, whether children profit from their experiences
abroad or suffer negative consequences depends on parenting.*
Given the challenges we face abroad ourselves, none of us
will be perfect parents. But we can take many steps that will
help. We can do our best to choose an assignment that suits
our children, to consider the impact on each child, and to be
ready to provide support. The ability to consider child-rearing as part of the adventure of going abroad is a great advantage. As children start picking up new behaviors and ideas,
our own ways of doing things will be called into question.
Bringing up children far from our usual support system also
confronts us very quickly with our strengths and weaknesses.
To be successful parents abroad, we make both an inner journey and an outer one.

Parenting abroad takes extra time and effort. Expatriate children need more support than children at home do. How
much they need depends on how difficult the move is for
each child and on that child's ability to cope. Parenting becomes more time-consuming because we become our
children's primary support system. In other countries many
of the sources of support we are used to are missing, and we
must take on new roles. Deciding how to be a good parent
also becomes more challenging. Our usual role models are
missing, and we are in an unfamiliar place. In Seoul, for
instance, what should children be allowed to do? What is
safe? Can we rely on what parents from other cultures decide? This can be viewed as an opportunity to make our
own decisions about parenting, but at the same time it can
be a heavy responsibility.

Sonja says, "In Yemen we had a lot of contact with people
because of the children. We were invited to people's homes,
and the kids were always more than welcome. Most Yemenis
really like children, and I think they could relate to us as

parents. It was a common interest. Friends without children had completely different experiences."

There are rewards for extra investment in children. Living
abroad provides opportunities for intensive interaction. Especially when they first go abroad, family members are dependent on each other for companionship, support, and
comfort. Even though they're all a bit stressed during this
time, it gives them opportunities to get to know each other
better and learn to face challenges together. Children are also
bridge builders in foreign countries. They bring us into closer
contact with people. They are less hesitant in approaching
strangers, and people also feel safer relating to foreign children than to adults and often treat them with surprising
openness. Children offer us new perspectives. They notice
details that we have overlooked and push us into considering different perspectives.

Responsibility

We choose *to go abroad; our children are* taken *abroad.* The question of parental responsibility is nowhere more extreme than
when we take our children away from their own country and
put them down somewhere else. All of us have reasons for
agreeing to go abroad. Not so our children. They mostly have
reasons for not going—just ask teenagers if they want to leave
their friends and go to the other side of the world. As adults
we also generally have some idea of what to expect, or at least
we are prepared to take a few risks as part of the price of adventure and a challenge. Children can be encouraged to face
such challenges but would rarely choose them.

*Children can't choose what is best for a family. That's our job and
our responsibility.* If we want to be honest, none of us go abroad
purely for our children's sake. We are happy if they see something of the world, become more open and develop some
cross-cultural skills, or can attend a private school, but these
are usually afterthoughts. Mostly there are career and material benefits and an opportunity for an interesting lifestyle.
Sometimes we assume that if it works for us we can make it

work for our children, and there's a lot of truth in this. Parents who are fulfilled and enjoy life tend to be better parents, but there are different consequences for each family member. Consider the situation of each member before each move. If children are old enough, ask them how they feel about a move and what their main concerns are. Take these concerns into consideration when making decisions. Older children should participate in decision-making.

With responsibility comes guilt. In interviews, expatriate women express guilt about everything that could conceivably be the result of taking their children abroad, from a child's dislike for chili to a broken limb. But even at home children have accidents, go through various crises, or need counseling. Feeling guilty when their children feel sad or depressed, some expatriate parents compensate with material goods and hesitate to refuse them anything. But children need reasonable limits abroad even more than at home, for safety reasons and to provide a sense of security. To thrive abroad, children also need a positive attitude, and we cannot encourage this if we feel overwhelmingly guilty about taking them there in the first place. Children whose parents feel terribly guilty may also refuse to take responsibility for their own behavior, blaming their parents for everything. This is tragic because although we can support our children, we cannot live their lives for them. Untimately they must take responsibility for their own decisions and behaviors.

Taking responsibilities seriously is a good antidote to parental guilt. If we honestly do our best to consider the needs of our children before each move and provide them with as much support as we can, we can more easily accept the consequences of a move, and children will be better prepared to handle any problems that arise. We must also accept the consequences of taking our children abroad. Living in other countries, they will try out different ideas and habits. Young children learn by imitating. It is not fair to get angry with them when they start copying the behaviors they see around them—when they mimic their nanny's mannerisms, for example, or adopt some host-country attitudes. Children's lives will almost certainly take a different path because of living abroad. In all likelihood, they will not settle down in our hometown and our grandchildren will not live around the corner. Children may choose an international career that takes them to the other side of the world, and multicultural children are more likely to meet and marry someone from far away. These are indirect consequences of the decision to go abroad.

Expatriate children are children of the future. We live in a world that is changing more and more rapidly, and children living outside their native culture can grow up ready and able to cope with global change. Our world is becoming increasingly multicultural, and the ability to relate to others who are different has become essential. As parents we have a duty to our children to do as good a job as possible of helping them not just to survive their experience abroad but to make the most of it. We also have a responsibility to the global community to help our children make the most of their privileges and become competent members of a global society.

Chapter 2
Moving Abroad

Wendy says, "When we went to Hong Kong we lived twelve stories up, with just a tiny balcony. I had to keep the windows closed and the balcony door locked all the time, because I was worried about the boys falling. There was no park or playground close by for them to play, and no other children living nearby. The kids spent all the time in the apartment. They never even learned to ride bikes. When we went to Nairobi, they just loved it. We had a big garden, and for the first six months they only came inside when it rained. Our house was quite close to the school, where they could go swimming, and there were other kids right next door. I felt like they were finally having a proper childhood."

Taking children to Kisangani or Timbuktu is not the same as taking them to Sydney. Where children live significantly influences their lives — whether they live in a large house or in a

small apartment twenty stories up, for instance. Health services, schools, and available activities are different in each
place. The culture is equally important. Children absorb what
they see around them, which will also affect, to some extent,
how they feel about themselves. In countries where foreigners are viewed with suspicion, children are likely to feel less
comfortable. Equally, they will feel more comfortable in countries that are welcoming of children—where children are
expected to be a bit noisy and are welcomed in hotels and
restaurants, and in people's homes.

Whether a place is "good" or "bad" also depends on the children.
At different ages they have different needs. A toddler needs a
safe place to play; teenagers need to have some independence.
For very lively children, living in countries in which this is
viewed positively—as a sign of temperament, for instance—
will be easier than living in places where they are supposed
to be quiet and well-behaved all the time. On the other hand,
shy children may feel more at home in countries where people
are reserved and keep their distance.

Choosing a Posting

The first time my husband and I moved abroad as parents,
we just went where the company sent us—to Saudi Arabia.
We found it a good place for youngsters, immensely welcoming of children and with a reasonable level of security
and medical care. We look back on our trips around the
Middle East as some of the most rewarding. When it was
time to move again, we had a choice of two cities and chose
Monrovia over Frankfurt—for reasons such as climate, clean
air, and our dislike of large cities, but also our own sense of
adventure. And adventure was what we got. The move to
Liberia was the beginning of several years in and out of
crisis situations in Africa. Our children still love Africa, but
in their interests we should have thought more carefully
about the potential hazards before we moved to that part of
the world.

Make choices carefully, if only for your own peace of mind. When we go abroad, if something goes wrong or a child has a miserable time there is always the feeling that "If we had hadn't made this move, this wouldn't have happened." Get as much information as possible about the new country. Consider all factors and make a responsible decision.

Factors to consider in choosing a posting:

- *Country-related factors:* the political situation, safety, medical care, climate, quality of life, specific dangers.
- *Situational factors:* where you will live (house or high-rise apartment), travel opportunities.
- *Child-related factors:* ages and needs in terms of schooling, medical care, entertainment, social life, activities, independence.

Some employees can go and take a look at a country before the move. This is an ideal way to get a feeling for a country. However, these so-called "look-see" visits are expensive, and many organizations offer information packages or videos instead. Unfortunately, a lot of the available material does not appeal to children. If you know people at a posting, ask them for information. Check the Internet. A great deal of detailed information about countries and cities is available. Schools sometimes make videos or CDs available. Most international schools have a web page. A friend's children found school yearbooks helpful.

> Vienna was an "It would suit our teenager" decision for us. It had international schools, an excellent public transportation system, and plenty of things going on. It is a relatively safe city, and our son already spoke German.

Each move will have different consequences for each child, depending on age, interests, educational requirements, and temperament. If children are old enough, discuss the move with them. Ask them how they feel about it and what their concerns are. What is most important to them? Are they worried about

being able to play football or about making new friends or
whether they will have their own rooms?

Factors to consider for each child in a move:

- *Age and level of development.* How will this move affect
  your 2-year-old or your 16-year-old? What do they
  need most at this age?
- *Available activities.* Will children be able to continue
  activities that are important to them? Are other activities available that may interest them?
- *How difficult is the move?* List the changes each child
  will have to make in terms of housing, schooling, and
  activities. Is this the first move? Have the children
  already made a lot of moves?
- *Individual temperaments.* How adaptable are your
  children? How do they respond to change?

Considering a posting and discussing it as a family takes time.
Unfortunately, organizations sometimes want employees to
make decisions quickly. If you need a few extra days to collect information and make a responsible decision, negotiate
with your employer. It is important that the whole family
come to terms with the idea of a move, and many organizations recognize this.

> Maya says, "When we went to Prague, all the kids found
> friends immediately and things they liked to do. Kurt loved
> playing baseball. When we moved to Vienna, Lotte didn't
> find any friends for ages and Kurt didn't make the baseball
> team. They were really unhappy for a long time."

*Even with the best planning, things don't always work out per-
fectly.* What counts is how we deal with the problems that
arise. It is often a matter of perspective, so keep an open mind
and think positively. Even bad points can be good. The lack of
TV in Liberia, for example, meant that our children spent very
little time in front of the screen and could watch only the videos we approved of. If parents maintain a positive attitude,
children are more likely to see things more positively too. Make

the most of what you have. If children are slow to find friends, for instance, take the opportunity to spend time with them and do things they enjoy. If they can't play a sport they are used to, perhaps it's a good opportunity to try something new.

Different Organizations, Different Circumstances

Very little in expatriate children's lives is untouched by the parent's employer — from the country they live in to the schools they attend. Within the international community there is a certain status associated with each job and organization. Often there is also a set of expectations associated with the children of employees, particularly in the case of missions, embassies, and the military.

Transfer Packages

When we accept a transfer package, we establish the framework for our children's lives abroad and must protect their interests. Look carefully at the conditions of the job offered. Check how your organization measures up on major points compared to other organizations. Clarify all points, and make sure everything that you feel is important is included in the contract. The nature of the employer also makes a big difference: whether it is a small company, a multinational, an international organization, an embassy, or a mission influences the circumstances in which children will live. (See the chart in Appendix A.)

> Joanna and John worked as missionaries in Kisangani, Zaire. When Joanna's mother was dying, a trip home to the United States meant delving deep into the children's college fund. Joanna was lucky that her family supported her and voted unanimously for the trip.

Very generous transfer packages are a thing of the past. Most organizations can no longer afford them. Think carefully about the financial package, especially if the trailing spouse can't work, as is often the case. The consequences of lower incomes are more significant abroad because expatriates often have to rely on expensive private facilities to compensate for deficits in housing, schooling, or social and medical facilities or because foreigners have limited access to local facilities.

The salary package:

- *Base salary.*
- *Foreign allowance* based on how difficult a country is to live in.
- *Mobility premium.* Some organizations award bonuses for willingness to move.
- *Cost of living index.* Most organizations pay a cost of living index based on costs for foreigners.

A package generally includes other benefits. Some organizations provide housing or pay a housing allowance. The cost of living is often higher abroad than at home. Apartments or houses in large cities are expensive. Expatriates often live in expensive areas because these provide accommodations similar to those at home, because embassies are located there, or because living in "expatriate areas" provides more possibilities for contact with others who speak the same language. Also, international schools are frequently situated in these areas. If you have to live far from your children's schools, either they will spend a lot of time on school buses or you will spend hours driving them to and from school. Some organizations pay the tuition fees for the school of your choice. Others will pay the lowest or offer a schooling allowance, with parents paying the rest if they choose an expensive school. Check what travel benefits are offered. Trips home are not a luxury but the key to a successful return.

Benefits:

- *Housing.* Is housing paid for, or is a housing allowance included? Occasionally electricity, telephone, or cable charges are also included.
- *Schools.* Is tuition paid for the school of your choice or the cheapest option, or is there a schooling allowance?

- *Health benefits.* Abroad you need worldwide insurance coverage. Does insurance also cover emergency evacuation? Some or all of these costs may be paid.
- *Freight.* What is the freight allowance for household goods? Some organizations also pay storage fees for items left at home.
- *Travel home.* Many organizations offer one trip home per year. In hardship postings, rest and recreation trips may also be offered.
- *Relocation assistance.* This benefit can include everything from practical moving help to assisting spouses in job searches.
- *Recreation.* Some organizations pay membership fees to a sporting or expatriate club.

> Thirteen-year-old Steven has lived in eight cities and six countries—he thinks. In any case, he has attended five different schools. After the most recent move, he didn't try out for teams or join any clubs. He said he didn't think he could make the teams anyway because he'd never really gotten good at anything, and he was tired of being the idiot who couldn't do anything right.

The effect of transfers on children depends on the length and pattern of moves. Is this a one-shot transfer or one of many? How long will you stay abroad? While most children can manage one two-year transfer, a lifetime of such moves can be a recipe for disaster. Educationally, such children often end up with "gaps." They do not have the opportunity to develop important social skills, and repeated transitions may cause lasting psychological effects.

> Alicia says, "When I look back at family photos of the years when we were moving around Africa really fast, the kids' faces are so serious. It's like there was just nothing to laugh about. I wish we could do it all over again."

Each move can leave family members feeling dislocated, negative, and isolated. Expatriate children who move every year or so often emerge from this difficult period just in time to pack their bags again. Fortunately, high moving costs have forced many organizations to work with longer transfer periods. Consider the length of the transfer when offered a job. If your organization is working on a contract basis, could the contract be canceled, requiring you to return earlier than expected? Can the normal transfer period be extended?

Some organizations mandate that expatriates return home at regular intervals. While there are good reasons for this, it can be difficult for children to switch between home and abroad. If the language of the home country is different from that used in schools abroad, this can mean several language changes during a school career—a serious handicap for most children. On the other hand, living in the home country from time to time enables children to maintain contact with their friends and extended family.

Parents need support if they are to successfully care for their children. There are large differences in the support expatriates receive from various kinds of organizations. Some organizations provide training courses before departure; families are met at the airport on arrival; and people are available to provide help when needed. Others provide little or no support. In interviews, some company directors said that if expatriates needed support, they should not go abroad. Actually, most of us *can* survive on our own, but the price in terms of stress can be high. If your organization takes the "tough it out" approach, be proactive: Read everything you can find about the new posting; contact expatriates who are already living there; and get in touch with expatriate organizations there as soon as you arrive. Accept the help offered by other expatriates.

Abroad, home must feel like home. Your home must be a place where you can relax and feel secure when everything outside the walls is foreign. Most organizations recognize this and expect to provide housing equivalent to an employee's former home or better, but there are differences in perspective. People in the head office tend to underestimate the problems of expatriates or think they are spoiled. On the other hand, expatriates are often suffering from culture shock and may be overly concerned with every detail. The most carefully chosen house can seem unsafe for a baby; having to take care of a blocked drain can seem like the last straw. Organizations should have clearly defined housing policies, recognize culture shock for what it is, and keep lines of communication open. Nothing beats the experience of having been in the same boat. Check whether anybody in the personnel department has lived overseas.

How much baggage will your organization pay for? You may be encouraged to take as few possessions with you as possible, but my rule of thumb is the more you take the better. A house or apartment should feel like home for children, and having familiar possessions with you is one way to achieve this. When we lost all our things when our house was looted in Liberia, it took a long time to create a "homey" atmosphere again. Transporting possessions around the world is a risk, so family heirlooms should stay at home, but not the familiar things of daily life, be they your everyday dinnerware, the children's toys, or photo albums. (However, to be on the safe side, keep negatives of photos and copies of family videos and important papers at home.)

Social Effects

Employers can also influence children's social environment. Military personnel who live on a base are physically isolated from host-country nationals and other expatriates. Some embassies discourage close interaction with host-country nationals in order to avoid conflicts of interest. Large organizations may provide activities or even schools, and their employees' children spend much of their time with children of other members of the organization. As a result, they have fewer opportunities to interact with different kinds of people or learn cross-cultural skills. However, children do structure their own experience to some extent, and many attend international schools that offer opportunities for cross-cultural contact. Parents can also encourage international contact by making friends from other cultures welcome, encouraging children to seek contacts outside their national group, and maintaining cross-cultural contacts themselves.

Conflicts of Interest

Not everyone gains equally from an overseas transfer. One parent is offered a job abroad and a range of benefits: higher salary, fringe benefits, career opportunities, job interest. If the family agrees to come along, this parent has little to lose. The advantages filter down to the next person in the chain, the so-called trailing spouse, usually a woman but sometimes a man, who also reaps the rewards of salary and benefits and the interest and excitement of living abroad. But the costs are already higher. If the spouse is working in the home country, the move abroad has a high cost in terms of career and status, although it can also provide a welcome opportunity to spend more time with the children. However, the spouse is still able to weigh the pros and cons of the move.

Children rarely have the chance to say yes or no. They are not good at weighing pros and cons. If you ask your children about leaving their friends or their swim team, you will rarely get a positive response. A private school? What for? Better social and cross-cultural skills? What's that? See the Eiffel Tower? Who cares? Parents decide for their children, and most of us are rightly torn between the idea that children are adaptable and the awareness that a move abroad is a major change in their lives.

Juggling family and career can be difficult abroad. Going abroad can often be a necessary part of the climb up the career ladder, but if career tops your list of priorities, it may not be the best move for your family. Many expatriate employees are expected to work long hours and travel a great deal, but expatriate children need *more* parenting rather than less. Discuss the situation with your spouse and set priorities. It is still possible to make career moves, but only if the needs of other family members are considered. Sacrificing family needs has a price. Spouses quickly start wondering what they are doing so far from home coping alone with children and the problems of living abroad. Many decide that if they are going to be alone, they might as well be back home, or even divorced. Children, too, are perceptive and may make short work of arguments such as, "We did it for you, for the good of the family."

Schooling is critical. Before children start high school, consider whether you will be able to stay abroad for the rest of your children's schooling. Will going home involve a language change? If possible, plan to stay in one place for at least the last two years of high school, as changes are very difficult at this stage. If you have to move during your children's high school years, try to keep them in the same school system. Plan your own moves to the extent possible. Few organizations manage good career planning, and almost none take children's schooling into consideration. Many transfers are actually quite haphazard and go something like this: "Oh, we need someone in Gabon in two months. Let's see who is available."

To plan transfers:
- *Start looking for jobs and transfer opportunities* at a time when it would be convenient for you to move.
- *Keep your ear to the ground* about jobs that may be coming up.
- *Let your boss or head office know that you are interested in moving* at a certain time.
- *If a suitable job comes up,* don't wait to be asked.

> Leif was offered a job in Brussels that he was loath to take. Financially it was not attractive, and the job did not appeal to him at all. However, the only other choice was to leave the company and move home to Sweden. If he did that he would not be able to afford a private school for his daughter. Now in her next-to-last year at school, she would have had to change back to a Swedish school, her fourth language change since starting school. Leif accepted the job.

Long-term expatriates can become "trapped" abroad by schooling needs. Organizations usually pay for private schooling abroad, but children are expected to go to public schools at home. For some children, this entails a change in educational system or language. While most young children can overcome this hurdle, it presents a major obstacle to children who are in their last few years of school.

> Rachael and Ivan were in a quandary. A job was coming up in Dubai, where there were schools for all four children — by no means a situation to be taken for granted. While this would be an ideal time to move their eighth-grade twins, who could start high school in the new place, it would mean moving their eleventh-grade son just when he was about to start his last year of school.

Perfect planning is difficult to achieve if there are several children in a family. While it may not be difficult to be fair to one child, getting it right for several children is almost impossible. What do we do if one of our children thrives abroad and the other is unhappy, or if two of our children are doing well in international schools and one is not? Obviously, we cannot make it right for everyone all the time. However, some needs are more important than others.

A child's needs take priority when the child:

- has a physical, educational, or mental handicap.
- is in the last year or two of school.
- has serious problems in the present situation.

> Thirteen-year-old Angie did not want to move to Cairo. She had friends at home and was involved in a lot of activities, but she said she'd go and have a look. Her father's company paid for only two people to go on a "look-see" visit, so Angie's parents bought an extra ticket for her. They visited the international schools, and Angie was impressed by the sports facilities at one of them. The school trips around the region were an added attraction. She decided that it

might be fun to live in Egypt, but she wanted to spend sum-
mers at home.

Balance out losses where possible. A summer camp can allow a
child to maintain a hobby or sport, for instance; tutoring in
school subjects or languages can help a child make a smoother
transition at school. Offer new opportunities such as trips to
interesting places with the school, family, or friends. Find fun
activities of some kind: amusement parks, concerts, sports. And
nothing beats extra attention from a parent.

Job Description

*The employee knows the job description and exactly what is in the
contract.* The spouse frequently does not. Not all organizations include spouses in pre-posting orientation sessions, and
some employees do not tell their spouse exactly what a job
entails. Sometimes they are afraid that the spouse might
refuse to move. Sometimes it is simply a sin of omission. Details get lost in the excitement, or the employee doesn't consider certain details important—not realizing that the
spouse's needs and interests are entirely different. However,
it is in the employee's interests to give the spouse a fair deal,
to keep him or her well informed, and to make family and
employment decisions based on all the facts.

> When they moved to Budapest, André did not tell Danielle
> that he would actually be away more than two weeks ev-
> ery month. After eight months of trying to cope with three
> young sons on her own, Danielle packed up and went back
> to Nice with the boys. Two years later the couple divorced.

When considering a job, find out how much traveling it will require.
Many expatriate employees are responsible for large geographic regions and travel a lot, leaving the spouse to deal
with the children. Some spouses can handle this or even enjoy
the challenge, but most would prefer a partner who really lives
at home. Bringing up children alone is more difficult abroad

than at home, and there is a lot less support. Constant comings and goings are also disruptive. Traveling spouses often want to move back into their family role when they come back from a trip, but home spouses, who have had to take all the responsibility in the meantime, may resent it. So do children. "You said I could go and stay with Angela tonight and now Daddy says I can't." Similarly, after a strenuous trip traveling spouses may crave peace and quiet, but so may home spouses, who feel that they have earned a break from the children. And children are looking forward to doing things with the traveling parent. Both partners should be prepared for the challenges of traveling assignments.

Chapter 3
On the Move

Sean's parents were not worried about their upcoming move to Budapest. Moving from Dublin to Taipei and then on to Dubai, their son had done well at school, made friends, and participated in lots of activities. Now that Sean was 14 years old and ready to start high school, it seemed a good time to move again—but Sean opposed the move from the start, and when they arrived in Budapest he hated everything. The weather was "depressing," the apartment "a poky hole," and the kids at school "dumb."

How we manage a move with children influences their adjustment. Taking them abroad is not necessarily unfair, provided that we don't move too often. If we take their needs and feelings seriously, they can profit from the experience, learning to manage change and new environments, which will help them later in life as well. However, ignoring their concerns can leave them with a backlog of anger and resentment. Without our understanding and support at each step along the way, children are far less able and likely to make a successful move.

Moving is not the same experience for children as it is for us — and it is a different experience for each child and at each age. A change of country affects a 2-year-old differently than a 16-year-old because each child is confronted with a different combination of challenges. As a result, there are no recipes for moving overseas successfully with children, but there are common factors. An overseas move—whether from home to a posting, from one posting to another, or back home again—is a major change for all children. Saying goodbye, leaving, and adjusting cause strong emotions — anger, frustration, loneliness, disorientation. These must be acknowledged and dealt with.

Preparing to Move

When should you tell children about an overseas move? When it first becomes likely or when you are sure you are going? There are good reasons not to get children excited or worried if you are unlikely to go, but they can quickly realize that something "is up," so don't delay a discussion too long. Children are quick to imagine something even worse—divorce, for instance. They also are often listening when we think they are busy doing something else, and their hearing is particularly acute if we are discussing something as important as a move to Bangladesh. If children ask what is happening, answer honestly. If you don't know yet, say so, and that you will let them know as soon as you do.

Keep young children informed and involve older children in decision-making. Discuss the move and get your children's feedback. Their reactions should be a factor in deciding whether to go or not. The things they are worried about, such as school or whether they will be able to play football, are issues that must be dealt with. Children need to feel that they have had a chance to express their feelings about a decision that will change their lives. They need to know that they have been listened to. If you decide to move even though your children have clearly said that they do not want to, explain why you made the decision. Involve them in other decisions—the choice of schools, for instance.

> On being told the family was moving to Singapore, Diederik bounded excitedly around the room, bombarding his parents with questions. His brother Floris was devastated; he stormed off to his room to call friends about the latest parental atrocity. A week later their positions were reversed: Floris was showing some interest while Diederik was having second thoughts about leaving his friends and his ice hockey team.

Children's first reactions to a move are unpredictable. Many things affect their responses: their age, the idea of leaving friends, or just the time of day. First reactions are often emotional. Children are excited, angry, indignant, or panic stricken. In the course of the next few weeks, they often go through a range of emotions: excitement at the idea of going somewhere completely different, sadness when they realize that they will be leaving friends, and anger at you for "doing this to them." Respond to these emotions rather than try rational arguments at this point. "I can see that you're upset at leaving your friends" will work better than "Yes, but we'll be able to visit other countries." Children are ready for facts once they have worked through their feelings.

Provide relevant information. When they are ready to really talk about the move, children want to know about the things that concern them: whether they will have their own room, what the school is like, whether there is a swim team. They are less interested in the population of the new country or the fact that the move is a great career opportunity for their father. This information often is not readily available, but international schools have web pages, and some can provide videos or CDs. Some organizations offer the services of relocation companies with contacts in your new country. Check the many web sites for expatriates or those with information about your host country. If you can go for a "look-see" visit, do so. If your children can't go with you, ask them what they want to know about the country so you can find out while you are there.

Give children things to look forward to. Consider what could be interesting, exciting, or rewarding for your children in the new country. Encourage positive expectations, but be realistic. Don't pretend that everything will be wonderful. When the children arrive and find that it is not like that, they will be disappointed and may stop trusting you. Answer questions and take children's concerns seriously. Involve them in the information search: "No, I don't know if the school has a volleyball team, but I have their e-mail address. Let's write and ask."

Take time to deal with your children's concerns, even though the time when you are preparing to move is likely to be very busy. If you don't have time at the moment that they want your attention, promise to discuss their worries at a more convenient time. Some children don't want to bother you, so if they don't come to you, make a point of asking them how they feel about the move. Ask children who have already been abroad to share their experiences with your children.

Expatriate children often feel that they have lost control over their lives. Someone has decided that they will move, and that's that. They feel helpless, angry, and frustrated, none of which will help them adjust well when they arrive in the new country. Put them back in control by encouraging them to make age-appropriate decisions—the kind of farewell they want, what to take along, what color their new room should be painted. Older children should have some say in school decisions.

Make the move as predictable as possible. Don't just have the moving company turn up at the door. Put a calendar on the wall so children know when things are going to happen—the farewell party, the last day at school, moving day, travel days, and so on. Even relatively young children understand the concept of three days until this and six days until that.

Moving is unsettling, and children often misbehave more just before a move, throwing tantrums or misbehaving at home or at school. Be understanding but firm. Relaxing the usual limits will only make children feel more insecure. Prepare small children for the move by acting it out with their dolls or toys. There are excellent books for children of all ages that cover everything from the mechanics of moving to the emotional reactions moving can cause.

Planning

With school-age children, timing is everything. Children should have time to look around and settle down before starting school, but not enough time to get bored and lonely. Avoid arriving at the beginning of summer vacation, when many expatriates go away. If you *are* arriving at this time, contact schools before they finish for the summer and ask them to put you in touch with children who are staying on, as well as available activities. Some international schools run summer schools.

> When we had to move in the middle of the year, our son's future first-grade teacher got all the children to write to our son and tell him how they were looking forward to meeting him. We still have the letters.

Try to arrive at the beginning of the school year, when schools and teachers make a particular effort to help new students. In international schools there are always a lot of new students at this time of year. Sometimes, however, it is not possible to choose your time of arrival. Organizations transfer people all year round, and while schools in the Northern Hemisphere start in August or September, in the Southern Hemisphere school begins in January or February. Fortunately, most international schools do their best to help children settle in, no matter when they arrive.

To help your children prepare to move:

• *Tell your children about the move* as soon as you are sure

you are going. Let them know important dates, what
day the packers come, the day you fly, and so on.

- *Provide relevant information.* Children want information
  about things that concern them. Involve them in the
  information search.

- *Give your children something to look forward to.* Get
  information about activities or fun things to do in the
  new country, but be realistic. Don't promise things you
  can't provide.

- *Take time to deal with your children's concerns.* Find out what
  is worrying them. Be patient with their fear or anger.

- *Let your children make age-appropriate decisions* — to
  choose what to take with them or the color their room
  is to be painted in your new home, for instance.

- *Try to time your arrival well.* If you can, arrive near the
  beginning of the school year, not just before summer
  vacation.

Goodbyes

Early in 1990 Monika and her three children boarded a plane
out of Liberia, fleeing a civil war. They never returned. Back
in Switzerland the whole family had trouble settling down.
Monika says, "The turning point was a trip to Canada to
say goodbye to our former neighbors and friends from our
time in Liberia. It was as if we could finally move on."

There are no good beginnings without good goodbyes. Ironically,
endings allow us to begin anew. Expatriates who are not able
to bid farewell to friends and places often find that they take
longer to get started again in a new place. Some adults who
moved a lot as children spend a lifetime dealing with "unfinished" emotions because they didn't have a chance to say
their goodbyes long ago.

*Always say goodbye, even if you are only going away for a year or
two.* When you return again, it will be to a new beginning.
We never pick up just where we left off. Things change. People
move away or find new friends, change jobs, drop hobbies or

start new ones. In a new environment we also change, developing new interests and skills. We become knowledgeable about African politics or Polish pottery. We learn to speak Greek. Even more significantly, our perspective broadens. We begin to see things in new ways.

Children change even faster. Children's best friends find new friends. Fads and fashions leave children behind, and they don't know what has happened to so-and-so on everyone's favorite sitcom. Children will also be in a different developmental phase when they return. Your toddler is ready to go to kindergarten, and your preteen is a teen with a new school and new interests. It is therefore important to prepare for a new beginning when you come home, and the first step is to leave in the best way possible.

Farewells

When our family left Zurich, our son's second-grade class gave him a T-shirt that all the children in the class had signed with textile pens. He wore it to bed every night for weeks.

Goodbyes are hard, and what's appropriate or popular is different at every age. Children often don't know how to bid farewell to friends, so discuss options with them. Do they want to go to their favorite restaurant with a few friends, or would they rather just visit a favorite place? Some children are shy about events and prefer private gestures such as giving their friends an address or friendship book or telling them in some way what the friendship has meant. Don't wait for others to organize farewells. People are busy or may not realize how important it is. In expatriate communities a lot of people may leave at the same time and friends may be overwhelmed. To avoid disappointment, ask your children what kind of farewell they want and organize it yourself.

Three-year-old Mikki walked around the empty house saying "Goodbye bedroom, goodbye kitchen." She ended with "Where's Mikki's bed? In the truck. Where's Mikki's horse? In Mikki's bag."

Have family farewells. Say goodbye to your house, call friends for the last time, have a last celebration dinner at home. Leaving is not only a sad occasion but also the beginning of a new adventure. Laughter and tears mix well.

Goodbye suggestions:

- *A farewell party,* sleepover, restaurant visit, or picnic
- *A farewell with a special group* such as a football team or a ballet class
- *Family farewells* with relatives or close family friends
- *Favorite activities,* such as going to the movies or on a picnic
- *Visits to favorite places* such as the beach, the mall, a playground
- *Private gestures* such as giving friends photos, mementoes, or address books; swapping e-mail addresses; asking friends to fill in "friendship books."

Sometimes we avoid saying goodbye and don't encourage our children to do so. We are uncomfortable with our own emotions or those of friends or children. We don't know how to respond appropriately, so we brush off children's grief and fears with, "Don't be silly. You'll be okay when you get there." Acknowledging that our children are sad also means facing our guilt about uprooting them. But it is this emotional work that allows us to build constructive lives in a new country.

Emotional Work

> I spent my childhood moving, but I only remember crying once. My mother got angry with me for it, and after that I never cried again. I still don't. Sometimes it's embarrassing, because people must think I'm really hard-hearted. Maybe my mother was feeling guilty or something, but I ended up feeling I had done something wrong as well as being sad and lonely.

Goodbyes cause painful emotions, sadness, anger, or frustration. Refusing to accept and work through these emotions does not make them disappear but causes them to be hidden away. When we deny children's emotions, we even prevent them from learning to recognize and name their anger, sadness, or fear. They are then unable to choose appropriate responses such as, "I feel hurt. Shall I tell my friend what is wrong, or stop being friends with him?" Instead, they simply react, driven by these emotions without recognizing them.

Emotional work is different at every age. Toddlers often release emotions explosively, crying or screaming or hitting out. Young children need help to identify the emotions and sort out appropriate responses: "I can see that you are feeling sad. Do you think it's because you are leaving your friends? How could you best tell them how much you will miss them?" Older children are more controlled, but even they can be overwhelmed by the strength and intensity of their emotions and sometimes need help to find appropriate outlets. Teenagers need an open ear and willingness to listen to their anger and frustration.

Children's friends will also be sad. Include them in talks about leaving, about feeling sad and missing people. Ask them to help your children keep up to date on what is happening at home. To save themselves grief, children's friends sometimes detach. They don't want to spend time with your children, and they start making other friends. Help your children understand that their friends are doing this because they *do* care. Encourage your own children not to let go too early.

> Ten-year-old Sandra says, "My friend Annette and I had this argument and we weren't talking to each other. Then Dad came home and said we were going to Peking. I was really excited, and I thought that that would solve the problem with Annette, too. Then I saw her at dancing class and she looked really sad, so I went up to her and asked if she wanted to make up. Now we write e-mails. She tells me what's happening at school and I tell her about some of the crazy things here."

A part of saying goodbye is dealing with unfinished business. Even children should start a new phase of life with a clean slate.

Encourage them to finish off with their friends, to express how much they will miss them, or to apologize, if necessary.

> Six-year-old Mediha stopped going to school one day. When her friends asked the teacher where she was, they were told, "She's left." One of the mothers says, "Now Naomi is afraid that her other friends are going to disappear. Every day she asks if they are leaving."

We cannot save our children grief. Only they can work through their emotions. If they are not given the chance to talk about and express their feelings to and for each other, they are less able to move on and may later suffer from unresolved grief. Unexpected exits frighten young children. If a playmate can disappear, they too, or other people they care about, could be snatched away. Although we cannot take away children's pain, we can help them move through the grieving process.

> Twenty-year-old Saskia says, "When Alan left to work in China, I cried for two days and then got on with things. My friends don't understand. They thought I would be sad for ages. It's the same when I see people off at the airport. I cry all the way home, and then it's finished."

Expatriate children do learn to manage grief. Many decide that it is inevitable, so they may as well go ahead and get on with it. As a result, they are ready to move on relatively quickly.

Preparing Goodbyes

When you move to a new posting, begin preparing goodbyes. In expatriate life someone is always leaving, and our turn often comes around all too quickly. Encourage children to maintain address books. Encourage them to write about experiences with their friends or to take photos. A keepsake or a photo from a shared experience can be a great gift when someone leaves, and stories and photos of friends help keep a friendship alive even when separated.

To help children say goodbye:

- *Create opportunities to express emotions* about the loss of friends, places, and activities at farewells, special events, or privately.
- *Help children identify, accept, and find appropriate ways to express emotions,* whether sadness, anger, fear, or frustration. Encourage them to tell their friends how much they will miss them.
- *Reassure children that grief is normal* and will not last forever.
- *Start thinking about goodbyes early.* As soon as you arrive, start preparing to say goodbye.

Traveling

When you turn the key in the lock of your old house, you step into limbo. You don't live *here* anymore and you don't live *there* yet. This is a heart-wrenching moment, especially for children. While you probably have a mental picture of the new place, small children in particular are only aware that home is gone. They saw it get packed up and disappear on a truck. Fortunately, young children let us set the scene for them. Mom, Dad, their teddy bear, and a goodnight story will often be enough to make things a lot better. Stick to normal routines and limits as much as possible. Special treats are great (being able to call and order room service, for instance, or swim in the hotel pool), but bend rather than change normal limits. Children need limits and guidelines even more in an unsettling environment.

Flying

Laura says, "I flew off to Gabon with our two boys. Brian had already started work, but I had waited until there was a house ready. I had 200 kilos of luggage. Thank goodness my parents live close and we could load up two cars. On the plane Patrick slept most of the way and John kept his

nose in a book. But with closing up the house and everything, I was still exhausted when I arrived."

Flying to a new posting is not an ordinary flight. It's a step into
the unknown, and for most expatriates it follows hectic weeks
of packing and farewells. If possible, spend a night or two in
a hotel before leaving, especially if you have a long flight or
are going to an undeveloped country where settling in will
be a challenge. If possible, both parents should set off to the
new country with the children.

Make flights as predictable as possible. Tell children what time you
will leave home as well as departure, arrival, and flying times.
If the children haven't flown before, explain about checking in,
boarding, and what will happen on the plane. There are excellent books for children of all ages about flying and airports. Involve children in the process: deciding what to take on board,
checking departure times on airport screens, or looking for your
gate. "Label" young children with their name, telephone number, and flight number in case they get lost in the crowd while
you are struggling with luggage and checking in.

Traveling with small children is challenging. Just keeping active
toddlers in their seats for long periods can be exhausting.
Take a night flight if possible. Choose toys carefully. (For example, if children are at the stage of throwing things, take
soft toys.) Select items that offer comfort or entertainment.
(We lost a lot of Lego pieces in planes and airports over the
years, but the hours of entertainment were worth it.) Ask
relatives or anyone else who is coming to see you off not to
give the children candy to minimize the chances that they
will get sick. Pack a few suitable snacks, as children's hunger
often doesn't coincide with airline mealtimes. Children spill
things and parents are favorite targets, so take spare trousers for yourself as well as for your children, if possible. Choose
drinks with spills in mind. I once arrived in Riyadh with red
wine splattered all over my trousers. (For once I was glad to
be able to wear an abayah.) Flying with older children is easier
these days. Planes offer a choice of movies and video games
around the clock, but in case they're not working, make sure

children have books or magazines to read and some kind of game to play.

> Five-year-old Charles, tired after the long trip from Singapore, where he had grown up, was horrified when his mother brought out some long trousers for him to put on before landing in London: "I don't want to wear long pants. You never said I had to."

Prepare your children for what to expect on arrival; they will be tired from the trip and less able to deal with surprises. Children think in details—where you will be staying, who will be meeting you, whether their toys will have already arrived. If you are moving to a country that is quite different from the one where you have been living, prepare your children for the way the people will look and how they are likely to behave—whether the airport will be noisy and chaotic, for instance. Talk about the new climate and the clothes they will have to wear.

To help your children cope with being on the move:
- *Stick to routines where possible.* Keep things as normal as possible in hotels or planes. Read the children's favorite stories. Play their favorite games.
- *Make arrangements as predictable as possible.* Tell your children where you will be staying and when you will be flying. If they haven't flown before, prepare them.
- *Involve your children if possible.* Get them to check boarding times and other information.
- *Prepare your children for their arrival.* Make sure they know what to expect on arrival, who will be meeting you, the climate, and so forth.

New Beginnings

You're there! Arriving in a new country is exciting and scary. Unfamiliar hustle and bustle, strange smells and people often overwhelm little children. Older children are more likely to be fascinated, but some are disappointed. It isn't what they imagined, or the letdown after the excitement of the past weeks is just too much: "I thought you said the weather would be nice"; "You don't expect us to get into *that* old taxi, do you?" Don't be surprised if they have picked up misconceptions, no matter how hard you tried: "Where are the lions/kangaroos/gangsters/movie stars?"

Arrivals are almost always chaotic. Everyone is tired but excited. Luggage is piled in a corner. Take a deep breath and try to create some order. When you arrive in your hotel or accommodation, unpack "home" things like photos, and dig out soft toys to put on the children's beds. Work out how to get the children back into a daily routine as quickly as possible. For the first week or so, go out and explore, but come back for mealtimes and bedtimes. Don't expect children to be too adventurous in terms of food yet, and have their favorite storybook and pyjamas ready at bedtime. Avoid getting too caught up in a social whirl the moment you arrive. Eat dinner with the children before going to a cocktail party. Put them to bed before going out to dinner. Refuse some invitations. People understand that children need their parents more when they first arrive.

A Honeymoon? Sorry, Don't Have Time

The first days or weeks in a new country are usually exciting, whether we feel frightened or fascinated. There are new experiences, things to see and people to meet. In the literature this is called the "honeymoon phase" because it often feels more like a vacation than normal life. Mundane realities have not yet set in. Children are excited by the new school and haven't yet faced the old realities of homework, friendship problems, or teachers they don't particularly like. The strong emotions of this stage are by no means all positive. Small children are often upset by the changes and don't want to let their parents out of their sight. Siblings may fight more than usual. Older children may be excited about everything, but only if "everything" includes activities and friends. If the new environment is not what they expected, they may be bitterly disappointed.

Take time to help your children find activities or to drive them
to and from places so that they can make friends. Not everything has to be unpacked immediately. Parents sometimes just
skip their "honeymoon." Moving with children is stressful, and
there are just too many things to be organized.

Culture Shock

Expatriates face culture shock. This can be expressed through a
variety of physical and psychological complaints, from tiredness and irritability to loss of confidence and depression. These
complaints are caused by the difficulties of adjusting to a new
environment. Children also suffer from culture shock, but their
problems vary according to age. Young children are likely to
be irritable and may take a step back developmentally. Teenagers may have angry outbreaks or retreat into themselves.
According to most studies, culture shock causes a downward
slide that lasts for a few weeks, with most people recovering
gradually until after six to eight months they are back to normal. Children's adaptation is less predictable. It can depend
on whether they find friends or activities immediately, for instance. Or, things will be great for a week or two, then suddenly they come home in tears. In general, teenagers take
longer to adjust because making friends and changing schools
is so much harder at this age.

Getting Settled

*New beginnings occur when we finally start to feel comfortable in
a new situation.* While adults tend to adjust slowly but steadily,
children's adjustment is more erratic. They react to individual
situations and events rather than to the situation as a whole,
and they can be happy one day and miserable the next. They
are delighted when they make a friend or find an activity
they like. But when something goes wrong with the new
friendship or they don't make the volleyball team, they are
upset or depressed.

> Patrick always stood on the sidelines for a while but settled
> in eventually. I could never quite identify the exact moment

when he started integrating, but one day I would notice
that he was doing well and getting invited places.

Children have different timetables for adapting. Some jump in
and take whatever comes. Others wait to get an idea of how
everything works before getting involved. In each place there
is a set of social rules: whether you have to ask to join in a
game of football, for instance, or how far you should stand
from others when waiting in line at the canteen. Children
who are slow to pick up the social rules in a new environment have the most trouble and may need help from parents, teachers, and possibly counselors to develop more
effective skills.

Every time we moved, Franzie would be in a group of girls
and it was all go, but I knew that within a couple of weeks
the cracks would begin to show.

New beginnings have their ups and downs. Children may make
friends quickly, then run into problems. The new friends may
not suit them, or as they settle down they begin to threaten
the group's leadership and be edged out. Making friends and
being accepted into social groups is a learned skill to some
extent. Children who have made many moves recommend
keeping a reasonably low profile for the first few months.
Discuss with children what they should look for in friends
and how to be good friends themselves. It can also take a
while to get involved in old activities or find new ones. Children may try out several new activities before they find something they like. Encourage persistence, but give them some
freedom to find out what suits them. Expect them to stick to
a new activity for a month or a semester, for instance; then
let them try something new.

Be sensitive to children's difficulties. Find a few minutes every
day to give each child your undivided attention. They will
often tell you what is wrong, or at least give you hints, if you
are really listening. Avoid offering solutions for problems too
quickly, but help them find their own solutions. "How do

you think you can deal with that?" or "How could you get to know Salwa better?" Provide logistical support, driving children to and from activities, keeping your home open to their friends, and supporting school activities.

At home children had mastered some aspects of their environment. Perhaps they could walk to a local shop. Teenagers may have been able to drive to school and to the movies. In a foreign country children lose some of this independence, at least until they can find their way around. Parents also restrict children's movements until they have found out what is safe, or because they are more nervous in a foreign country. As a result, children often feel helpless and frustrated. To reduce these feelings, help them master the new environment, whether it's teaching a 3-year-old how to open the doors in the new house or helping a 15-year-old use the public transport system. Explore the neighborhood and city with your children. Make sure they can use the telephone and know the emergency numbers and what to do if they get lost.

Foster a positive attitude to school and the host country. Avoid talking negatively about your new country or criticizing the school or teachers. Celebrate each new beginning and success. If children get onto a team or join a new activity, celebrate in some way. When they make new friends, invite those children to dinner. Children often have trouble seeing beyond today and their present problems or feelings. Reassure them that things will get better: "I understand that you don't enjoy this ballet class as much as the one at home, but I think it will be better when you get to know everybody. Would you like to invite some of the other children home one afternoon?"

Watch for problems. If children seem to be taking a long time to settle down, or if those who usually adjust well do not seem to be happy this time, ask teachers for advice. In international schools classes are generally small and teachers get to know their students well. They see many children go through the adjustment process and often know when a student is not adapting well, and they can offer suggestions and help.

Coping

When children overcome obstacles, they often gain a sense of mastery. Even small successes, such as getting onto a new football team or just successfully using a few words of a new language, can give a sense of satisfaction. Help children learn to appreciate their achievements in the new environment. Be ready to celebrate these successes.

> When Michael's father's company lost a contract, his mother agonized over how to explain to her son that they would have to move again after only eighteen months in Malawi. She was surprised when he said calmly, "Mom, I know how to change schools. I've done it before. I'll manage."

Although moving is always tough, many expatriate children learn to "hit the ground running." They know how to find their way around new schools. They jump straight into activities and are good at making new friends. At 14 our daughter read me her list of ways to make friends in a new place. Recently I picked up a book for teenagers on moving and found a very similar list — written by a professional who had conducted years of research. Our daughter's advice: Keep a low profile initially; listen as much as talking; ask for advice; accept invitations to join groups or activities; be prepared to make the first move when necessary; keep looking for friends when things don't work out initially.

> Veronika, an ESL teacher at a school in Vienna, was worried. Even after three weeks, the two Chinese brothers in her class had not spoken a word. The 9- and 11-year-old boys seemed totally overwhelmed. Eventually she discovered that their father had set them up with an apartment and bank account and left them on their own while he conducted business around Europe.

Challenges must be reasonable. Children can gain a sense of mastery only if they are not overwhelmed by the problems they face. Although dealing with an occasional failure is also a lesson in resilience, repeated failure is not healthy. Children need support if they are to turn the challenges of an overseas move into lessons in mastery.

Some children cope too well. They try to spare us extra worry when we are busy, as is inevitable in a new country, and do not tell us they are having problems. If your children are the kind who always help out or look after others, don't take their smiles at face value. In the adjustment phase, set aside time every day to give each child some attention even if they seem to be coping.

To help your children settle down well:

- *Anticipate culture shock.* Expect the children to take time to settle down.
- *Encourage your children to take up old and new activities.* Allow for false starts.
- *Listen and offer sympathy* rather than advice.
- *Help your children regain independence* in the new environment.
- *Foster a positive attitude.* Avoid negative input.
- *Watch for problems.* Children should be challenged but not overwhelmed.

Chapter 4
Special Issues in Parenting Abroad

Barbara notes, "I'm glad we brought our children up abroad. We always had to think about what we were doing with them. I think we must have done some things well because we have a good relationship with them now—but it wasn't always easy. We never knew if we were doing the right thing, and there was no one to ask. I used to talk to my mother about things when the kids were small, but she didn't know anything about the places where we were living. I talked to other expatriates and read a few books. We stuck to basics, but sometimes we were just winging it. It's worse with teenagers. They want to go places and you don't know if it's safe. They often made fun of me because I was nervous, but they wanted to do things that I'd never done, so of course I was scared."

We want our children to grow up to be balanced and fulfilled adults, but how do we achieve this when living abroad? They are growing up in a foreign environment. As parents, we encounter situations that our parents never had to face. Because our children face special challenges, they have some different needs from those of peers at home. We want to bring them up in much the same way that we were, but we don't have these cultural models in front of us. Instead, we are surrounded by different ways of raising children. How do we decide what is the best? How do we deal with other people's criticisms when they think *they* know best?

Abroad we also become the sole keepers of our children's well-being. Our extended family can no longer provide support. Some social institutions are not available because of language or because as foreigners we are not entitled to their services. Services that we are used to are missing, or we don't know where to find them. In Japan, for instance, we can't just look in the phone book for a party service or a sports club. At the same time, expatriate children need more support than ever as they adjust to new schools and find new activities and friends.

Norms of Child-Rearing

Sylvia says, "I wanted the kids to learn proper table manners. I didn't want them to have trouble when they went back to England, but they said they would look like dorks if they behaved the way I wanted them to at school. Then one summer we stayed with my sister, and her kids didn't have the kind of manners my mother had taught us either. I guess things have changed."

Bringing children up the way we were raised is instinctive. It is what we are familiar with and what we believe in, to some extent. It is what we consider normal, and it will help our children fit in at home. As a result, most expatriate parents try to raise their children in much same way that they would at home, but this is not so easy. How *are* children brought up in our country? At home, first-time parents are guided by what they see around them or by their families. For expatriates, these models are missing and we have to rely on what we remember, but our memories are often incomplete. We may have vague ideas about discipline, but should we remove dangerous items from children or should they learn not to touch them? How should we deal with tantrums? Things have also changed at home. Do parents still insist on "please" and "thank-you"? And we live in different circumstances. How can I teach my children the rules of fair play when no one else on their teams believes in the same rules? There are also new situations. If children are growing up bilingual, for instance, is it polite to let them use a language that others don't understand?

> I found my moms-and-toddlers group exhausting. Everyone was from a different country, and there were really big differences in how we expected our kids to behave. We all tried to be nice about it, but we were all protective, always watching. I never knew what to encourage Nikki to do. Compared to some kids he seemed really aggressive, but with others *he* was the one who always seemed to get pushed around.

Abroad we are surrounded by other ways of bringing up children. A few expatriates spend most of their time with people from their own culture, but mostly we're with people from different cultures, and so are our children. This gives us a lot of ideas about different ways of raising children and causes us to question what we are doing. Moreover, there probably is no other subject that is more emotional for us than our children. In a multicultural situation, differences in how we bring up children are not academic but affect the children directly. Nada tells our son off for being too noisy. Mara lets children at her house watch adult movies. Rosario's mother lets the children ride their bikes on the main road when they play at his house. Your daughter's best friend is not allowed to come to her birthday party because her parents are afraid that you won't supervise the party well enough. And how do you respond when a mother in a play group thinks it's okay for the 2-year-olds to hit each other and says, "They will sort it out?" Will they? Do you want your child to start behaving this way? Will he be disadvantaged in this group if he doesn't?

Often we don't understand other people's reasoning or don't see the whole picture. For instance, in the preceding example the mother did actually interfere if the children looked as if they might hurt each other. People often have good reasons for their behavior, so try to get more information about their attitudes. Ask questions: "Do you think they can always deal with it?" "Don't you think they need some help sometimes?" Let people know where you stand. "I worry that one child will get hurt or that they won't

learn to share." Ask friends how children are raised in their countries or to explain why they do something in a particular way. If
you are part of a group, start a discussion about different options.
Seek compromises. It is important to be tolerant of others but equally
important that they be tolerant of you. As a last resort, find another
group that suits you and your child better.

Criticism

> I used to get offended when Jordanian friends corrected my
> son. As far as I was concerned, they were interfering and im-
> plying that I was not a good mother. Then another friend said
> that I should be flattered, that it meant that they had accepted
> responsibility for him. I didn't get as upset after that, but I still
> didn't feel very comfortable.

*Abroad, friends and strangers alike may criticize our way of bringing up
our children,* from a gentle question to a lecture about what we are
doing wrong. Sometimes people simply want to understand. In
other cases they just assume that their own way of doing things is
correct. Expressing or not expressing criticism is also based on
culture. Criticizing others is common practice in some countries,
and is accepted or countered. In some cultures, bringing up children is a community task—and therefore everybody's business.
In English-speaking cultures, child-rearing is generally considered a private affair. Most parents are offended when someone
criticizes them. Abroad, if you are criticized, try opening a discussion: "Is that how people do it in your country?" You will
learn about other ways of doing things while reminding the other
person that your ways are different.

> In Liberia, our driver was shocked when I asked him to pull
> over until our son stopped screaming. "But he's a boy," he
> said. "He should be strong (willed)." For a split second I re-
> ally wondered if I was being too tough. It was quite strange
> because back in Switzerland he would have been jumped on
> swiftly for behavior like that.

*What children are praised for in one culture they may be criticized for
in another.* This makes child-rearing challenging for expatriate
parents, but the truth is that you will never be able to satisfy

everyone around you, so do what you think is best. Be prepared to ignore criticism when necessary. On the other hand, it does offer food for thought.

Different expectations are also confusing for children. Children try to adapt and, fortunately, usually learn to use different behaviors in different situations, but they do make mistakes. They sometimes need help in deciding which behavior to use when. In various cultures people say "Hi," shake hands, kiss cheeks, or hug, and children may not be sure which greeting to use for whom. Do not punish children for responding "wrongly," but make your own expectations clear.

The Golden Middle Way

> I really didn't know what to do. All the kids at school seemed to meet at the pubs on the weekend, and Alicia really wanted to go. At home kids aren't allowed in bars until they're 21, and Alicia was only 16. She said she was the only one who was not allowed to go. I didn't want her to go, but I didn't want her to stay at home every weekend on her own, either.

Our children are growing up abroad. They need to be able to do as well in their present environment as they did at home. We cannot put them in such different situations and expect them to grow up just the same as us, or as children at home. To do so puts everyone involved in an impossible situation. We must decide what works best for our children and for us by considering each situation on its own terms. If the children are old enough, discuss it with them. Negotiate compromises.

> Where Nellie was growing up, children were expected to play quietly. She remembers her young cousins spending many of their waking hours in a playpen, but she says, "I studied psychology at university, and I thought children should be able to explore their environment and to be treated as real people, to be listened to. I'm so glad my children have grown up abroad. I don't think I would have dared to do things so differently if I'd been at home. My mother doesn't always approve, but she adores the kids, so they can't be turning out so bad."

The expatriate situation is an opportunity for more aware parenting. Seeing other ways of doing things, or having our children behave differently, forces us to think about our own child-rearing methods. As a result, we are less likely to blindly bring up our children just the way we were raised but to search for the best path for our children and for ourselves. However, this is hard work. We constantly have to consider options and make decisions. To help us, a lot of information on child-rearing is available. And if we foster a close relationship with our children, we are better able to make decisions that are in their best interests.

Not everyone welcomes this freedom. The insecurity of living abroad sometimes causes people to cling to everything associated with home and be fearful of anything different, including ways of raising children. Such people may put pressure on other parents from their country, putting them in a difficult situation. If you find yourself in this situation, show understanding for your compatriots but do what you think is best for your children: "I know you think our children should be in bed at 8:00 at night, but we find that in this climate they need to sleep during the day instead."

To find a child-rearing path abroad:

- *Consider raising children abroad an opportunity for more conscious and aware parenting.* Keep an open mind. There are a variety of methods and ideas out there.
- *Consider your children's situation.* Find compromises.
- *Help your children learn appropriate behaviors* for home and abroad. Be patient with mistakes. Be clear about your expectations.
- *Be tolerant and expect tolerance* from others.

Children's Friends

Anita says, "When John's friends call, they are often not very polite by my standards. One child used to call and just say 'John?' When I complained, John protested, 'Kanako hardly speaks English, Mom.' When Kanako called from then on, I said, 'Would you like to speak to John?' to kind of show him what to say."

Friendships are an important part of children's lives and social development. We should encourage friendships and make our children's friends welcome in our home, but this can be an adventure. Friends come from other cultures and have different ways of behaving. Their manners are often quite different from ours. This can be disconcerting when children walk in and inspect your whole house, for instance, or drink their soup straight out of the bowl. It can also be rather nice—when you are treated with great courtesy, for example. My children's Arab and Asian friends never fail to come and say "Hello" and "Goodbye," and their Swiss, German, and Austrian friends shake my hand when arriving and leaving.

Children from other cultures are used to different sets of rules. This creates the dilemma of what to allow or forbid in your home. One guideline is safety. In some cultures children are allowed to do things that we consider unsafe, but you are responsible for what happens in your home. In my house, for instance, children never played with matches, and in my car they were asked to wear seatbelts. Ask your children to help you develop guidelines. They can be very insightful and often understand their friends better than you can. No matter what rules you eventually decide on, always treat other children with respect and kindness. Remember, your children will be in the same position at other people's homes.

> Jamini's mother was worried about letting her daughter go to a friend's house. "They are American," she said, "and he works for the drug people. They probably have guns in the house."

Ask other parents if there are things they don't want their children to do. If they are worried about what their children do in your home, they may stop them from coming. Address sensitive issues. Parents of Muslim, Jewish, or Hindu children, for instance, may be worried about what their children might eat in your home. Sometimes other people's fears are based on stereotypes about different countries or on rumors they have heard. An open discussion can help. If possible, get to know the parents of your children's friends. It is easier to discuss issues if you have a good relationship, and we tend to be more tolerant of people whom we know and like.

To support children's friendships:

- *Promote your children's friendships.* Making and keeping friends is an important part of children's social development. Make their friends welcome in your home.
- *Ensure children's safety.* Protect other children in your home. Discuss safety with your children's friends' parents.
- *Treat other children with respect and kindness.* Even if they do things differently, treat them the way you would like your own children to be treated.
- *Get to know other parents.* This builds trust and makes it easier to solve any problems that arise.

Support Systems

To provide children with support, we must have it ourselves. We rely on many sources of support in raising children, not only friends and family but also all the services that help us cope with our children, from medical services to people who organize children's birthday parties.

A support network generally consists of:

- *Friends, family, neighbors.*
- *Official support systems:* schools; medical and social services, including various forms of testing or referral services; support for disabilities; and so forth.
- *Informal support:* community support and facilities, commercial services for children.

When we move abroad, we become our children's primary support system. Often we must leave our support network behind. Some or most of the services we are used to may be missing, or we don't know where to find them, or they may be inaccessible because of language problems. Fortunately, much of the "support gap" can eventually be filled, but it remains our job to identify the resources in a new country and to coordinate them. Where possible, contact some resource people before you leave home and others as soon as you arrive. Some organizations pay relocation companies to help you settle in. These have personnel in host countries who should be able to help you find what you need.

> Evelyn says, "Two days after we arrived in Lusaka, both kids got ill. I didn't have the name of a doctor to call and had no idea where the hospital was. Luckily, there was an American lady living down the road. She put the kids in her car and we drove to a clinic she knew. I don't know what I would have done if she hadn't been there."

Get in touch with other people and organizations as soon as you arrive. There is a lot to do when you arrive, and it is tempting just to get on with it, but you need to build up a support network as soon as possible. This is especially important for spouses. Employees go off to the office, children to school—and spouses are left home alone. In most cases other expatriates are the first source of support. They can provide practical advice as well as social interaction. For parents, schools are often a place to meet other parents. In most major cities there are groups of expatriates, such as international spouses' groups or American women's associations (also open to non-Americans) where you can meet other expatriates. Accept any help that is offered. Even if you don't really need it, it's a good way to get to know people.

Start a file of names and addresses. Wherever you go, pick up business cards or write down the addresses and phone numbers of services that people recommend. Note whether your language is used or only the local language. Arranging to have family photos taken, for example, doesn't require much language, but a child psychologist should speak your language fluently and have a good grasp of your culture. Embassies usually have a list of approved doctors.

Your file of support facilities should include:
- *Medical services:* doctors, specialists, dentists, psychologists, psychiatrists, medical laboratories, X-ray clinics, physiotherapists, and alternative medical specialists such as massage therapists, chiropractors, and so forth.

- *Support services:* national and international groups; expatriate services such as emergency call-up services; training.
- *People you meet.* Who was it who mentioned that they knew a good dermatologist or where children could go roller-blading? Keep a notebook with you so you can write down names and numbers.
- *Translators:* people who are willing to translate when you need it.
- *Helpful services:* babysitters, party services, a seamstress, a photographer, costume rental.

In most countries there are useful services that don't exist at home, and discovering them is one of the interesting aspects of living abroad. In Saudi Arabia a friend organized a belly dancing teacher for her daughter's 11th birthday party, and the most beautiful birthday cake my son ever had was made by a baker in Kinshasa. The best classes on music appreciation for children and adults alike were, not surprisingly, in Vienna. Consider services that are not so common at home—acupuncturists in China, for instance, or masseurs in Hungary.

Keep your own records. You are on your own and will have to keep your children's school, medical, and dental records. Each time you leave a place, ask for your children's records. If you live in an unstable country, keep a copy of these records outside the country.

Support from Home

Maintain contact with home. Especially in the beginning, we need to know that "home" is still there. Budget for telephone calls, write letters, and make installing e-mail a priority. Let your children make a predetermined number of calls home. Share your experiences with people at home. Send tapes and videos or small, interesting gifts. Sometimes friends and family members at home are not very supportive. It may be a matter of "out of sight, out of mind." Often they can't relate to our lives any more, or they think that we have a wonderful life and are envious. They may feel that we are not taking our share of burdens such as looking after aged parents. Try to bridge the gap. Don't just write about the "wonderful trip to Paris" or the "trip to Victoria Falls"; write about the realities of living with power and water cuts or communicating in another language. Discuss how you can continue to take a share of home responsibilities. Remind others that you often "do your share" in intensive bouts, such as when you are visiting or when others visit you.

> When my son was suffering from the aftermath of war and evacuation, I could not get our pediatrician in Switzerland to recommend a therapist. "What do you expect if you take your child to those countries?" was his reaction.

Some people consider taking children abroad irresponsible. Even professionals such as doctors may fail to differentiate between careless and careful parenting, ironically making responsible parenting more difficult. Instead of giving you the health information you need, they may give you a lecture on your foolishness. If this happens, change doctors. Find a true professional who will take you seriously and provide the support you need.

To cope without your usual support network:
- *Contact people before you leave home,* if possible, or find out whom to contact as soon as you arrive.
- *Build support networks as soon as possible.* Collect information about people, services, and organizations.
- *If you are offered help, accept it.* Even if you don't really need it, accept help if it is offered. It is a good way to meet people.
- *Keep your own records.* You are now responsible for your children's support network. Keep track of their school and medical records.
- *Keep up contact with home.* People at home don't always understand, but they are an important source of support.

Chapter 5
Family

Annette says, "I know we haven't always done the right things. Sometimes I think I haven't been as good a mother as I would have liked, but when I look at families at home, I am really happy with ours. Even though they've left home now, the kids keep coming home. They call often, and we know pretty much what they're up to. We were really involved in their lives—maybe too much sometimes, but when I look at families at home, they're just so casual. It's like family is just something you grow up in and then leave. It's not enduring. But it is for us."

When we move abroad, we become the ultimate nuclear family, often thousands of kilometers away from extended family, friends, and other support systems. At the same time, the family becomes the mainstay for expatriate children. In the absence of friends, it becomes more important, a major source of support and comfort and the one thing that stays much the same while everything else changes. For many expatriate children, family members are the only people who have shared their experiences in various countries. Building a strong and durable family therefore is an important part of parenting abroad.

Family building has physical and emotional components. We must create a physical home for children abroad, a place in which they feel comfortable and safe. Even more important is creating a caring environment so that children can grow up healthy and confident, sure that they are loved and cared for. Creating a home for our children against a changing background is not easy, but we have a number of tools that can help. We can create a physically pleasant place to live no matter where we are. We can work at generating a warm and comfortable family atmosphere and give our children the security of predictable limits and a set of family traditions that provide a sense of continuity. We can work harder than usual at "family" skills: communication, understanding, negotiation, and supportive discipline.

Family Systems

Our family is the community we create with our partner and our children. It is the human environment we provide so that our children can grow up feeling physically and emotionally secure, enabling them to thrive as children and to grow into healthy adults. But what makes a good family community? How can we make it work well for us and for our children? Living abroad puts special demands on the family. The family is the only continuous community in the lives of expatriate children. They participate in other communities, such as school or expatriate and local communities, but these come and go. Whether a family "works" or not becomes more important when children are less able to rely on other forms of support. At the same time, expatriate parents will not find much information or advice on how to cope with their special circumstances.

Moving to Bandar Seri Begawan was a nightmare. I couldn't work any more and Michel, who had always been an independent child, suddenly got really insecure and didn't want to go anywhere on his own. Even getting him to school was a problem.

The family is a living community. Part of building a stable family is being responsive to change. Children grow and change, and every move abroad brings additional changes. We may live in different circumstances—in the middle of a city rather than in the country, for instance. Spouses can often no longer work. Children who grow up with other cultures also pick up new behaviors. All these factors change family dynamics. To constantly readjust, family members need to keep in touch with each other—to communicate, share feelings and ideas, negotiate and work out compromises. Although children need stable guidelines and routines, these must be flexible enough to accommodate changes. Family rules, for instance, aim to protect children, but when we move to another country the dangers change and so must the rules. For example, a family meal may change from evening to midday if you move to a country in which everyone goes home for lunch. Responsibilities within the family will also be reassigned with each move. Spouses who are no longer working usually accept more family responsibilities, but these need to be discussed. If they move from a place with household personnel to one without, children usually have to take on more household chores.

Family Styles

To thrive abroad, children need to be capable, self-confident, and tolerant, and *our* parenting style must reinforce these traits in our children. According to studies that have been replicated many times and in different ethnic groups, the so-called *authoritative* (not to be confused with *authoritarian*) family is most successful in raising children to be confident, self-reliant, and socially competent. These children also achieve well and are least likely to have behavioral or psychological problems.

[Authoritative parents] have firm and clearly defined limits, but encourage age-appropriate autonomy. They encourage their children to have their own opinions, are supportive and involved in their children's lives. Home is organized, with predictable routines.*

In expatriate situations, this kind of parenting presents special challenges. Each move changes circumstances, and limits must be renegotiated. Teenagers who are used to going out on their own at night, for instance, may no longer have the same freedom in another, more dangerous city. Or they may be able to buy alcohol, which they could not do at home. How we encourage independence will also vary from one place to another. Children can learn to make good judgments and decisions no matter where they are, but it takes some thought to provide appropriate opportunities for them in different countries. Responsiveness to children and their opinions, as well as involvement in their lives, is perhaps the best tool for expatriate parents. Our children are growing up in a different environment and can easily grow away from us if we do not keep up with their development.

Protecting the Family

Living in another country and culture is stressful. Don't wait for problems to develop. Children need to find outlets quickly, so make finding some physical activity a priority. Have fun. When everyone is beginning to get upset, ignore the unpacked boxes and find something fun or relaxing to do.

Tabea says, "I think my husband and I survived so long overseas because we just kind of picked each other up. If I'd had a bad day, he would take the kids out into the garden for a while or something, and vice-versa. We tried to teach the kids that you should treat the people you love the

* Baumrind, Diana. "Authoritarian Vs. Authoritative Parental Control," *Adolescence*, vol. 3, no. 9 (Spring 1968). Baumrind has written many articles on patterns of parental authority and the rearing of competent children. Many other researchers have replicated her research.

best and not the worst. It didn't always work, but sometimes it did."

Family members can provide support for each other. Moving affects every member of the family, but we don't usually all have
a bad day at the same time. Successful expatriate partners are
usually adept at giving each other support. Talk about helping
each other, and model helping behavior with children. Even
small children can understand others' needs and learn constructive ways to respond. It doesn't mean that siblings won't ever
fight or take their bad temper out on each other, but it does
create a mindset. Our daughter used to say, "Having to put a
smile on your face for someone else usually makes you feel better too," and she recently stumbled on some research that ap-
parently showed that the brain registers and responds to smiling
with an outpouring of "good mood" neurotransmitters.

Reserve time for family. Family gatherings, whether mealtimes,
outings, or family meetings, are a time for everyone to express emotions, get support, and talk about experiences.
People change fast in new environments, particularly children, and it is easy to lose touch with each other even when
living in the same home.

Build other support groups. Support groups take pressure off the
family. Take opportunities to meet people, collect phone numbers and e-mail addresses, and invite people home. Encourage
your children to find interest groups. Initially the groups you
find may be expatriate ones because it is easier to communicate
and they welcome newcomers and understand the problems of
settling in. Studies show, though, that in most countries people
who adapt well also have local contacts and friends.

To build a strong family system:

- *Be sensitive to change.* Each move brings changes. Be
  prepared to renegotiate roles so that everyone is
  comfortable.
- *Use an authoritative parenting style.* In a foreign environment it is important to have clear guidelines but to be

flexible and prepared to renegotiate when conditions change.
- *Seek stress relief.* Take time for relaxation. Encourage family members to support each other.
- *Reserve time for family.*
- *Build other support groups.* This helps the family and takes pressure off the family system.

Family and Continuity

> Sangeeta is 40 years old. As the daughter of a diplomat, she spent her childhood moving from one country to another. "I think of my childhood as a series of boxes piled up on top of each other. There's not much to connect any of them—a few letters, a memento or two. I was never able to call my friends or visit them again. I feel like I was a different person in each place, and I can't relate to the 'me' in old photos."

Moving does not have the same implications for adults as it does for children. It means an adjustment for us, but for our children it can affect every aspect of development. Young children, for instance, have a limited sense of continuity. People who disappear from their lives have, in a sense, "died." Older children know that their friends still exist but may find it difficult to maintain contact without help.

> Carla says, "My Mom is the only one who understands how scary it is to cross a road in Teheran, have shoes go moldy in Africa, and visit relatives in Mexico who think we're all weird."

Family provides stability and continuity. Parents and siblings are part of children's lives through all their various postings and experiences. We can reinforce this continuity by sticking to similar family guidelines and routines in each place. In a new place, keep up important family rituals. If you can't have the family meal at the time you are used to, for instance, find sometime during the week when you can all eat together.

Family traditions can be celebrated anywhere. For children's birthdays, the home and the country don't matter as much as the cake, candles, and birthday songs. A Christmas tree in Saudi Arabia can be a decorated houseplant. Pack a few traditional items, or improvise. Create new traditions such as goodbye rituals, or celebrations for the first day in a new house or at school. A tradition or two from each posting is a good way to integrate experiences from abroad. For stepfamilies, new traditions create common ground.

Family traditions can take many forms:

- *Family events* such as birthdays.
- *National and religious holidays.*
- *Special meals* such as ice-cream sundaes on Mondays.
- *Family customs* such as watching a movie together on Saturday nights.
- *Rituals* for leaving and arriving, the first meal in a new home, or the first day of school.

Help your children keep track of their lives. Because they sometimes have trouble putting the pieces of their lives together, use timelines, photo albums, or journals to help them tell the story of their lives. Encourage your children to maintain contact with friends and family. Younger children are not very good at keeping up long-distance contact and may need help. Set up e-mail accounts and encourage them to write. Make videos and tapes to send to friends and family. Encourage them to display photos of friends and family members.

Some expatriates keep a house or a holiday home to return to during vacations or between overseas assignments. In this way children can keep in touch with some of their friends and attend the same schools. Unfortunately, for financial reasons houses often have to be rented while the family is overseas and are unavailable when needed for short stays. Many expatriates also want to explore the part of the world they are living in rather than going home. Sometimes children can treat grandparents' homes as a point of reference. When my

mother moved house following my father's death, our children said they felt they had lost their home in New Zealand.

To provide continuity for children:

- *Stick to familiar guidelines and routines.*
- *Keep family rituals or create new rituals,* such as celebrations
  for new beginnings or goodbyes.
- *Encourage your children to maintain contact with friends
  and relatives.*
- *Help your children develop a sense of their lives* — with
  personal timelines, for instance.
- *Develop stable points of reference.* A residence in the home
  country, grandparents' homes, vacation locations.

Family as Home

Melanie says, "Wherever my family lives is home for me.
They just moved to Prague. Since I'm in college I will never
really live there, but as long as they are there, that will be
home. After I haven't been home for a while, I start to get
homesick. I start calling more often."

We do not deprive children of a home when we take them abroad.
Home is not a specific set of walls or an exact geographic
point. It is the experience of safety and comfort and the care
we can give to the people we love. In many ways, the family
can become home for an expatriate child. But not all children feel the way Melanie does. Some do not develop a sense
of the comfort and security associated with home and grow
up feeling that they don't have a home at all.

The atmosphere in a home is more important than the actual house
or apartment or even the country. For children, whether their
environment feels like home or not will depend on whether
their house or apartment is a place of safety, warmth, and understanding. As adults, we can walk into an apartment or house
and make it a home. Children cannot do this. They first have
to experience safety and comfort. "Home" is a concept that

children must develop before they can create their own homes. People who grow up without this schema tend to feel as if they are constantly on the run and surrounded by dangers. When we create a home for our children, we give them something for the future as well as the present.

Abroad, home should be a place of refuge for every family member. Teenagers can be difficult, but parents should not, even at the height of an argument, threaten to "throw them out of the house." In a foreign country our children have nowhere else to go. There are no grandparents or other adults to run to. In many cases children do not yet have friends to whom they can turn. For expatriate children, "home" must be irrevocable.

Apartments and Houses

Housing is more important abroad than at home. When everything outside is foreign, home should be a place you can retreat to, where things are familiar. In some ways we have to be able to create our own country and culture at home. For this we need a place that is comfortable and secure. In a new country most people are more nervous than at home because they don't yet know the dangers. They need more security than otherwise. Saving money on housing is therefore risky. Before going abroad, make sure that your organization recognizes the need for adequate accommodation. Find out what they offer in the way of housing advice or assistance. Some organizations provide housing. This certainly makes things easier initially, but it means that you can't choose what best suits you and your family. If you are living in a potentially dangerous country, pay special attention to security.

Take the time and effort to turn a house into a home. We know that our stay will be limited and this may be our fourth or fifth home, so it's tempting not to put up pictures or buy a mat for the floor, but children need a home, not just a house or apartment. It doesn't have to look like an illustration in a beautiful homes magazine. More important is that the children's pictures are hung up, that they have a place to put their toys and a place to play. Some people start making a new place theirs at the most basic level by cleaning it from top to bottom. How you stake your claim depends on your budget. But whether you hang up original paintings or posters, customize your four walls and let your child do the same.

> The workmen painting Joanna's new apartment in Turin nodded knowingly when she said that one child's room should be blue and one pink. "Ah," they said, "Pink for the girl and blue for the boy." Joanna found it easier not to explain that it was her daughter who wanted blue and her son pink.

Children also need to stake their claims. Let them organize their own space. Young children can tell you where they want their things. Older children can sort out their own rooms. Offer to help, but do not insist. Their rooms may not turn out to be your idea of "homey," but it is important for them to feel that their space is their own. If a room needs to be painted, let the children choose the colors, or they can pick out curtains or a piece of furniture. Give older children a budget for things for their rooms, even if only for a few posters. Older children, especially teenagers, need privacy, and their rooms should be places they can retreat to.

> Shirley has lived in six African countries. She says, "I try to make myself at home as quickly as I can so that I don't spend a long time feeling lost. I have a duck ornament—quite silly really—but when I put that somewhere, then I am at home. My children do the same thing. My son is in college now, but he made sure that he took his stuffed piranha with him. My daughter takes her coffee mug everywhere."

Most people have items that symbolize home to them, from family photographs to a personal coffee cup or mementos. Identify the items that need to be in place for you to feel at home, and take them with you. They are useful shortcuts to creating the mindset that a house is now home. Encourage your children to have their own symbols.

To create a sense of home for your children:

- *Make housing a priority.* Choose comfortable and secure housing. This is your place of retreat when the foreign environment becomes overwhelming.
- *Make a home of your house or apartment.* It is important for children to have a home. Spend the time and effort needed to personalize your space.
- *Encourage your children to personalize their own space.* Let them choose the color their room is painted or buy a few posters.
- *Use symbolic elements* such as family photographs.

Chapter 6
Raising International Children

Helena says, "When we first went abroad, I was really worried about Leif. He was a difficult baby and didn't like change at all. We've moved three times and it hasn't always been easy. He takes time to settle. But he's really well-balanced now—for a 16-year-old, anyway—and he thinks that living abroad is great. The other day he was on a chat line with a cousin at home who's just a bit older and was shocked that she's already planned out her life in the town where she's always lived. He said, 'There's so much to do in life. She's missing all the adventure.' I thought that was interesting because if we had stayed at home I'm sure he would have become one of those people that never want to move."

In many ways, international children are made and not born. How well we do abroad as adults depends to a large extent on our personality and abilities. For children it is the other way round. Their personalities are influenced in many ways by their experiences abroad. In an overseas environment they are more likely to become adaptable and tolerant, for instance. Of course, temperament is also a factor. Children who can sleep anywhere, eat anything and communicate with everyone will adapt more readily. Older children have relatively well-developed personalities before they go abroad. But given parental support and encouragement, almost all children can adapt to this lifestyle, becoming more flexible and outgoing than they would be if they had stayed at home.

Living abroad can be a growing experience for children. Not only can they survive without serious negative effects, but the experience can enrich their lives. "International" skills and abilities such as adaptability, tolerance, and resilience help them thrive. Parents can help their children develop the skills and abilities that will enable them to make the most of their stay abroad as well as acquire skills for the future.

Succeeding Abroad

Expatriate children need to succeed abroad, because there is a lot at stake. When we go abroad, we already have fully developed personalities. Even if we hate living abroad, it is just an unfortunate episode in our lives. But children's experiences abroad affect their development. What happens to them in various countries becomes part of their sense of self. Doing well abroad therefore is even more important for them than for us. Part of parents' job is to help children develop the skills that help them thrive in their new environments. Learning to get along with people from other cultures is not a luxury but a necessity. By living in other countries, children meet people from other cultures on *their* territory. Meeting people from Ghana or Oman or Belgium in your own country is not the same as going to live in their countries. Most expatriate children attend international schools that typically have students from as many as fifty different nationalities.

To do well abroad, children need to develop resilience and self-esteem. In foreign places they may make a lot of mistakes. Unfamiliar with the host culture, they don't know what is expected of them. If they fail to greet people when they walk into a shop, they may be scolded for being rude. The lady at the movie theatre speaks so fast that they can't understand her, even though they've practiced what to say. At school, there are different rules about interacting with teachers and students. Their friends come from different cultures and have different expectations of friendship. At home, we get upset with them when they adopt new behaviors learned at school or in the host country.

Expatriate children must find the courage to try new things, new activities to replace those they cannot continue in their new home, or new skills, from catching a bus to speaking a new language. In the beginning, life abroad is a series of mistakes and frustrations for children. They need confidence, healthy self-esteem, and persistence to face these challenges.

International Skills

The skills that help people abroad are often listed as character traits, and organizations sometimes test for them in an effort to predict whether employees are likely to succeed abroad or not. Children, however, are still in the process of development. With encouragement, they can all develop these traits or skills. Indeed, studies show that children who have grown up abroad *are* adaptable, can relate to different kinds of people, and are able to take different perspectives. Parents can help children develop these "international" skills and abilities, thereby helping them make the most of their international experience and also preparing them for an increasingly international world. Of course, expatriate children are not the only ones who develop such skills. Parents who raise their children in a tolerant atmosphere and encourage them to be open to differences and to cope well with changes also prepare them to become "international."

Traits of an "international" personality:

- *Skills needed to cope with a multicultural environment:* adaptability, social and communication skills, tolerance

for ambiguity, and tolerance for differences.
- *Personal abilities:* resilience, self-esteem, persistence.

Adaptability

> Alicia hardly recognized her son when she saw him eating
> with his friend's family at the school picnic. She says, "Adam
> was using chopsticks to down his food. When I went over
> to join them, he was being so polite to Jee-Ah's parents. I
> didn't even know he had manners like that. I hope some
> more of Jee-Ah's manners rub off on him."

Abroad, an adaptable person accepts differences on many levels,
not just adapting to the physical changes of moving to a new
home, but accepting differences in behavioral mores and, at
the deepest level, different belief systems. Children are more
adaptable than adults. Young children in particular learn primarily by observation. They "see" more than adults, notic-
ing even the smallest details in their environment; this
enables them to copy others and therefore behave more appropriately in the new culture. And young children don't
see anything strange in different ways of doing things. While
we might find many things in a new culture inappropriate,
bizarre, or even disgusting, young children just soak up what's
around them. Even older children, though more likely to consider certain things "weird" or "gross," are more open to new
impressions and ideas than adults. As a result, children pick
up new ways of perceiving, thinking, or behaving more
readily than adults.

Children make mistakes when switching cultures. Although children learn how to behave in different cultures, they don't
always know when to use each behavior they have learned.
They don't understand why they can't do things the same way
as their schoolmates or friends: "Why do I have to eat like
this. It's much more comfortable at Tom's house, where I can
put my elbows on the table." Help children understand that
there is a place for different ways of doing things. Negotiate
compromises. A friend insists on "her" manners at home, for
instance, but allows different manners when she cooks food from

other countries. Her children are learning that different countries have different concepts of what is appropriate.

To promote adaptability:

- *Encourage adaptability.* Avoid criticizing your children when they try out something new. Admire their ability to adapt.
- *Be patient with mistakes.* Some confusion is natural.
- *Help your children behave appropriately.* Help them understand which behaviors can be used where and when. Make your expectations for specific situations clear.
- *Seek compromises.* Your children are living in a different environment. What will work best for them, and for you, in this situation?

Social and Communication Skills

Most children master new social skills faster than adults do. The tools of observation and mimicry that nature gave them so that they could learn to live with others are an asset abroad. They observe how others are behaving and are quick to notice, from people's reactions, when they have done something wrong. These skills are very important in adjusting to a new country and to new schools, where there are new norms of behavior. Children who are sensitive to social cues adapt faster. After a few weeks in a new country, you often can't pick them out in a crowd because they've adapted to the local body language. They know how far away to stand from people and what gestures to use. If children tell you, "You can't do that, people here don't like it," they're probably right.

> Heidi had taught her 6-year-old son to shake hands with Swiss friends, but she noticed that he did not look at them. "You must look people in the eye when you shake hands," she told him. "How long do I have to look at them?" he asked. She thought about it and then told him three seconds. She says, "After that, I could see him silently counting to three, but at least people don't think he's rude when we go home."

There are exceptions. Some children have trouble fitting in, even at home. Less sensitive to communication cues, they have difficulty picking up new social rules. They touch others in ways that are considered inappropriate, or cannot judge how assertive to be in various situations. These children need extra support in an international environment.

Parents can promote social and communication skills. Encourage children's powers of observation: "Oh yes, that car does have a foreign license plate. Where do you think it comes from?" Airports are great places to play games, from "Who is the first to see a lady with a red skirt?" to "Can we pick out the Americans/British/French?" Use "Pick the accent/language" to check who was right! Help children identify and practice social behaviors. Dressing up for different events or talking about what is appropriate to wear or do in a variety of situations helps children develop awareness of different customs. Discuss what clothes are "in" in different countries. Practice the expressions that match emotions or role-play social situations. Charades are a fun way to practice these skills.

To promote social and communication skills:

- *Use games and activities* that promote observation and social skills.
- *Teach or model essential skills if necessary.* If you notice that your children have not "picked up" a necessary behavior, practice it with them or model it, in a fun way, if possible.
- *Watch for children who may be having difficulty.* Seek professional help if necessary.

Tolerance for Ambiguity

Tolerance for ambiguity is the ability to cope with unclear situations. When that man waved at us, for instance, did he want us to come or go away, or was he being rude? Being comfortable with *not* knowing is an essential skill abroad. If we get upset every time we don't understand exactly what is going on, we will soon have a nervous breakdown. Children are also constantly faced with such situations. In international schools, there are dozens of nationalities and a lot of scope for misunderstandings. Out on the street, they often don't understand why people do things and may lack the language skills to find out.

Children are more accustomed to ambiguous situations than adults. They are just learning how the world works, and for young children even things at home can be confusing. As a result, they are more capable of just going with the flow. However, they don't have the tools we do to reduce ambiguity — to read about the new country and culture, for instance. They need our help to make more sense of their new environment. Share your insights into the host culture or the expatriate community with your children.

If you accept ambiguous situations, your children will be more at ease. Admit when you don't know why something happened. Speculate about why things might have happened: "I really don't know why that lady got angry. I wonder if she didn't like me standing so close, or was she just having a bad day?" Avoid culturally negative interpretations such as "People here are just rude." If you are unnerved by a situation, say so: "It makes me uncomfortable when I don't know what I am supposed to do." Your children undoubtedly feel the same way at times.

To promote tolerance for ambiguity:
- *Reduce ambiguity.* Help your children understand their new environment.
- *Demonstrate tolerance for ambiguity.* Stay calm, speculate, but avoid negativity.
- *Express discomfort.* Admit when you are uncomfortable, but avoid blaming it on the environment.

Tolerance for Differences

Fifteen-year-old Charles was miserable at his new school. Proud of his nationality, he did not understand why others did not admire his country too. He found his schoolmates ignorant of the things he considered important and just couldn't relate to their sense of humour. The others teased him mercilessly about his national pride and his accent. Friendly and outgoing at home, Charles became angry and defensive.

Expatriate children fit in better if they are comfortable with other cultures. Few expatriate children can spend all their time with people from the same culture or nationality. Even American children in an American school or British children in a British school can find themselves in classrooms in which the majority of children are from other cultures. Out on the street, all expatriate children are a minority. They are the foreigners. Being able to accept other cultures makes life easier and more rewarding.

Tolerant children find it easier to adapt, find friends, and get involved. International schools are usually small, and there often are not many children to choose among in making friends. It helps if children can get along with all sorts of people. Other children are also more accepting if they feel accepted themselves. The ability to relate to different others also helps children be accepted and feel comfortable in the host country.

Children learn tolerance by experiencing tolerance. When we accept our children and try to understand them, even when we don't agree with them or they develop differently from the way we are, we are giving them a lesson in tolerance. We increase the chances that they will show the same understanding of others. Accepting our children the way they are is more challenging abroad because they are exposed to many different ideas and are more likely to develop differently. But even when you don't agree with them, take them seriously. Initially their ideas may not be well thought out or may be very dogmatic. They will develop more balanced views in time, especially if they have opportunities to discuss issues.

Sylvia says, "When we moved to Ireland, I told my husband, who's English, that he wasn't to tell any more Irish jokes because the kids were going to local schools and I didn't want them repeating anything offensive. He stopped, but they had already gotten the message. Harry said, 'If everybody in England thinks like that, the jokes must be true.' He doesn't think that anymore, but it took ages."

Children will follow your example. They watch how you behave toward the people around you, so avoid moaning about the "locals" or indulging in cultural jokes. It is an easy way to get rid of frustration over feeling like an idiot in a foreign country, but try not to express negative stereotypes around children. They pick these up without recognizing that they are partly just a way to relieve tension.

To promote tolerance:

- Foster a warm and accepting environment at home.
- *Be prepared to discuss issues with children.* Listen to their ideas and arguments even when these are not yet well developed. Encourage children to consider various perspectives.
- *Model tolerance.* Avoid being negative about people from other cultures.

Confidence and Self-esteem

Sixteen-year-old Alona says, "When I came to school two years ago, I didn't understand anything. I really wanted to learn English, but it took a long time. I was better than everyone else in the math class, but sometimes I got things wrong because I didn't understand the instructions. One girl always made fun of me. She got everyone laughing with her, and then they would just look at me like I was really stupid. I felt like going home and never coming back."

To get through the adjustment phase, expatriate children need a robust sense of self. When they arrive in a new country, they are the new kids at school. Even the system and language may be different. Out on the street it's just as bad. They don't know how to use the bus system, or they can't ask anyone for directions because they don't speak the language. Young children, especially, have few tools to help them get used to new countries. They can't read a map or use a phrase book. Children who feel sure of themselves not only survive this phase better but adapt more readily. They are willing to ask questions, start conversations, or just try out something new. As a result, they can find their way around, make friends, and find new hobbies and activities more easily.

Parents can promote self-esteem in their children by encouraging their interests and talents as much as possible. They protect self-esteem when they shape behaviors through encouragement rather than criticism, by being positive when children do something well rather than negative when they do things wrong. Support and sympathy during the adjustment phase help children master the challenges and give them the confidence to get through difficult situations or master new skills.

To promote confidence and self-esteem:

- *Support interests and talents.* Help your children participate in activities they are interested in or find new activities.
- *Shape behaviors through encouragement rather than criticism.* Be positive when your children do something well rather than negative when they do things wrong.
- *Give your children support in difficult times.* Provide support and encouragement to help children face the challenges of moving and transition.

Resilience

Expatriate life is full of hard knocks for children. Some can hardly communicate with others for the first few months in a new school. Out on the street, they may be unable to ask for the simplest thing in a shop, or they may be yelled at for doing something wrong. Expatriate children must be resilient, able to bounce back and be ready to try again.

Steve says, "Laurie hated it when we came here. We are stuck in the middle of the jungle, really. Then I noticed that butterflies fascinated her, so she and I started hunting them. She didn't like the idea of killing them, so we take photos. We go to all sorts of places near here. When we get too hot, we come home and jump into the pool."

Positive thinking is a shortcut to resilience. If children see living abroad as an adventure, they are more likely to see themselves as privileged rather than disadvantaged. They will almost always find things that they like and enjoy. However, particularly at the beginning of an assignment, children may need help in finding activities that they like because many of the things they enjoyed before have disappeared and they cannot conceive of new ones. Start by focusing on small things: being able to pick up shells at the beach, having a playground close by, being able to buy 100 different ice-cream flavors.

Tomorrow is a new day and a chance to start over. This is obvious to us, but it often isn't to children. A bad day can seem like the end of the world: "Marie is angry with me. The teacher hates me. I never want to go to school again." Help children put things in perspective. "You can apologize to Marie. Ms. Baker was just upset because you were talking when you shouldn't have been." Give children things to look forward to — "We're going to the movies tomorrow." Distract them with a game or a book, or share your day — "Something really silly happened to me today."

Tanja says, "When we first went to Dubai, Alex settled in really well but Bojon didn't, because he got really ill. I felt bad because they're twins. I wanted to tell Alex I was really proud of him, but what was I going to say to Bojon? Then I realized that he was doing fine too, just taking smaller steps, taking more time. I think it helps if kids feel they don't have to achieve too much at once."

Expatriate children spend their lives learning new things. This is frustrating, and they need support when they feel like giving up. Children need to know that it is normal to have to try over and over again. It is not always easy to find activities that they like, so let them try out different things, but encourage them not to give up too easily by setting the condition that they continue until the end of the month or semester, for instance. Help children consider every step along the way a success: making a new friend, hitting the ball once, trying out a new activity. Celebrate small successes with a favourite meal, watching a special TV program, or a trip to the zoo.

Welcome extra support. Other adults can help children integrate into a group, encourage them to try something new, or just be there to talk to. Children need someone to confide in. With all the stresses of moving abroad, you can't always be that person. If your child is having problems, let a teacher or group leader know. Sometimes just a little extra encouragement can make all the difference.

To promote resilience:

- *Encourage positive thinking and a sense of adventure.* It is important for children to consider themselves privileged rather than disadvantaged. Start small. Liking a whole country is too much to ask in the beginning.
- *Expect your children to try out various things before finding what they like.* Let them try out new things, but encourage them to stick to each thing for a specified time.
- *Remind your children* that tomorrow is another day.
- *Celebrate each success.* Help children appreciate even small successes or steps on the way to a larger goal.
- *Welcome support.* Other people can also give our children support and encouragement.

Independence

Maria says, "When we went to Harare, I was scared to let Nicola out of my sight. I heard lots of stories, and I didn't know what to believe. She was really upset with me. At home in Athens, she used to go all over the city with her friends. Eventually we let her go out with friends here too, but only with our driver or the driver of one of her friends."

In Western cultures independence is an important goal of child-rearing. We expect our children to become increasingly independent and self-reliant. Becoming independent is particularly important for expatriate children because they constantly face unfamiliar situations, and they need to be able to think independently. Friends come from many cultures with different rules and social norms, and children can't rely on their judgment or the consensus of their social group. But it can be difficult to encourage independence abroad because we are unfamiliar with the country. How do we know whether it's safe for children to go horseback riding in Kinshasa, to a disco in Nicosia, or to a bar in Vienna if we don't know these cities and have never done these things ourselves? We also hesitate to let children do things because we don't understand local systems. We won't let them take public transportation, for instance, because we don't know how it works. We can't explain the system to them, and we know that if they get lost they can't ask for help because they don't speak the language.

Most of us are nervous in new countries. "Mom and Dad don't let me do anything on my own any more," Paul complains when his parents won't let him do the things he was used to doing at home. We ask other parents, but people from other cultures often have different ideas of what is appropriate for children at different ages, or they are even more (or less) concerned about safety than we are. Children also lose previous competencies because *they* don't know how things work or are nervous about doing things that they used to do at home. At the same time, they need to be more independent and self-reliant than at home.

What Is Independence?

Shirley and Ron were very proud of 18-year-old Shaun. He had adapted to Paris well. He spoke passable French and had friends of many nationalities with whom he went all over the city. When Shaun went to college, they were astounded when the uncle he was living with wrote that Shaun was not very independent, complaining that Shaun didn't know the first thing about getting a job and had to be driven everywhere because he didn't have a license.

Our children often don't develop the skills associated with independence at home, but they can do other things. They can fly across the world alone, even if they can't drive or operate a bank account. They can make complex decisions about cultural identities and solve cross-cultural conflicts, even if they don't know how to behave at a party at home. However, sometimes they become *more* dependent as a reaction to a new country. Wendy hates it when her parents go out at night, something she didn't mind before they moved to São Paulo. This is usually temporary and disappears when children master the new environment and learn new things.

Adults often equate independence with the things children are able to do. Children think it's about the freedoms they are allowed. But independence is more than either of these. It is children's ability to assess situations and make rational judgments on their own, as well as the ability to stick to these judgments even when others think differently.

Independence and self-reliance involve the following skills:

- *Accurate judgment of situations, people, and one's own abilities.*
- *The ability to make good decisions.*
- *Enough self-confidence to trust one's own judgment and put decisions into action.*

These are general skills rather than specific activities, such as driving a car or operating a bank account, and it takes longer to learn them. The skills associated with driving, for instance, can be learned relatively quickly, but adolescents are not really independent until they can use a vehicle responsibly and with proper consideration for others. Learning to make such judgements and decisions can be accomplished abroad, even if driving cannot.

Children need practice in making good decisions, so provide age-appropriate opportunities as early as possible: Let your children choose their own clothing, manage their pocket money, make decisions about activities or school courses. They learn as much from mistakes as from doing things correctly, but it is better to make mistakes with pocket money than with a credit card, for instance. When your children make a bad decision, help them identify what went wrong: "I understand that it is difficult for you to go out with your friends if you don't have any pocket money left. How could you manage it better next time?"

Freedom!

"Freedom" is a big issue, especially for teenagers. For teenagers, independence means being allowed to do things without adult supervision. This presents us with a special set of problems when we go abroad. What should we allow them to do? What is safe? We often hesitate to allow adolescents to do things in a new country, and they usually resent this. Most are proud of the independence they had at home or at the last posting, and they resent losing it.

Decide what mistakes children can afford to make. If you don't know the country very well, allow freedoms first in areas in which miscalculations won't have serious consequences. Allowing children to decide which new items of clothing they need most, or to choose their own courses at school, cannot become life-threatening. Letting a child take at taxi late at night could be. Let children know that you need time to work out what is safe. In the meantime, provide logistical support, picking children up from a party, for instance. Encourage children to do the things that you know are okay, such as taking the school bus or walking to the corner store. If children could take public transportation to friends' houses but are too scared to do so, go with them until they become more confident.

> Edith says, "When we moved to Vienna, I was worried about the boys going all over the city by public transportation, but I don't worry so much now. They seem to handle things well, even dealing with ethnic gangs or other young people asking for money. The police stopped Simon recently because he was running home late at night to make his curfew. He obviously handled it fine with his bit of German and didn't even seem worried about it."

Discuss situations with your children. They have a strong interest in their own safety, and although their judgment is not perfect, they are often more mature than we give them credit for being. Consider each situation individually. Should you stop a 15-year-old from going to a party where teenagers are chatting, watching videos, and listening to music just because there are also drunken parties? Discuss each event with your children and other parents. Is there going to be alcohol? Are parents going to be at home? Who else is going? Trouble can't always be predicted. Tell children that you expect them to come home if the party turns out differently than what was agreed.

Get accurate information. Ask local people what they allow their children to do. They may have different criteria. Some cultures are less concerned with safety, for example, but you can allow for this. If you are worried about swimming pools, sports facilities, movie theatres, restaurants, discos, or bars, visit them yourself. Make sure your fears are well-founded. Make a list of the things you are afraid of and get information about each. Avoid using fear as an instrument of control, as in "You don't want to worry me, do you?"

Children must be able to contact you if something goes wrong. Mobile phones are very effective in lowering stress. Parents can check that children are okay, and they can reach us, or someone else, if they need to. "Hey, Oliver, I'm lost and no one around here speaks English. How do I get to your house again?"

Prepare for emergencies. Agree on emergency procedures in
the event of something going wrong. What these are depends
on the country. In some cases children need to have the telephone number of the embassy, for instance. Have the name of
a lawyer in case your children get into trouble.

> I was helping our son's 16-year-old friend register for a sail-
> ing course because he didn't speak German. Rani met me
> off the train, chatty and pleased to have something to do
> during his vacation. Registering for him, I noticed that he
> suddenly did not look nearly as confident or happy. He
> was obviously embarrassed to have me doing something
> he would do himself at home.

*Encourage your children to gain a working knowledge of the local
language,* at least enough to regain some independence: asking for tickets at the movies, finding their way around, giving basic information when asked. Language is also a factor
to consider in moving with teenagers. Living in countries
where they do not speak the language limits their independence to some degree.

The Goldfish Bowl Effect

> Seventeen-year-old Paul got drunk at an expatriate club in
> Singapore. The next day several people called his parents,
> and the school heard about it as well. After being told off
> both by his parents and by the principal, Paul was furious.
> He told his parents that he felt like he was living in a gold-
> fish bowl and wanted to go home to a "normal" life.

Expatriate communities are often like villages. Everybody knows
everybody else and meets at the same places. As a result,
children often can't do anything without us eventually hearing about it. Teenagers resent this situation, but for parents
it is an opportunity to provide children with more guidance,
discuss bad decisions with them, and possibly help them avoid
even larger mistakes. But we should treat the situation with
care. If you hear stories about your children, ask them for
their side of the story (not all stories are accurate). Give them

the opportunity to tell you what they could have done better and what they plan to do if the situation arises again. If you hear of an embarrassing rather than dangerous incident, keep it to yourself.

Knowledge

Knowing a host country gives children independence. It helps them get around and understand people. And the more you understand people, the easier it is to be positive about them. I can get angry at the lousy driving I encounter in some countries, but having local friends who drive exactly the same way makes me more accepting—and careful! Equally, having a reasonable knowledge about their home country gives children independence when they go home on vacation or when they return. Children learn best by doing. Going places is one of the easiest ways to learn about a country, both at home and abroad. Of course, teenagers might not be very interested in the cultural delights of cities either at home or abroad, so try taking turns—something for you and something for them. This will offer you some new experiences: water world, a games center, an unusual exhibition or a jazz bar, for instance.

Maps are passports to freedom. They help expatriate children get around in foreign cities and at home. Small children need customized maps as they have trouble with the two-dimensional and symbolic features of maps, but 3-year-olds can relate to a map with photos of their house and neighborhood. Older children can use maps to get around the city or give you directions. Get bus or subway maps if children are getting around on their own.

To promote independence:

- *Give your children opportunities to make age-appropriate decisions.* Children need practice in making decisions. Help them learn from their mistakes.
- *Help your children gain confidence in their judgments.* Help them recognize and appreciate when they make good decisions.

- *Find opportunities for your children to learn skills.* Decide what mistakes they can afford to make. To find out what is safe for children to do, get as much information as possible. Encourage your children to take advantage of opportunities to learn new skills.
- *Be available when things go wrong.* Make sure your children have your telephone number. Get mobile phones if possible.
- *Make sure your children are well informed* about both the home and the host country.

Chapter 7
Special Families, Special Challenges

The Jackson five—Bill and Pat; Marianne (15), Sandy (13), and Adam (10)—moved to Paris six months after Bill and Pat married and took custody of Bill's children. When they were barely settled, Bill was off traveling for six months of the year, leaving Pat to deal with the children. Pat organized birthday parties and kept in touch with the children's teachers, but she felt as if she was constantly "running to catch a train she had already missed." Marianne began staying out until all hours and engaged Pat in regular screaming matches. Sandy became withdrawn and fell behind in school. Only Adam did well, developing a good relationship with Pat. Bill, struggling with his own job, was unable to deal with the problems at home. Three years later the family moved home, but not before Marianne was sent to boarding school after throwing a chair at Pat, and Sandy had lost a year at school.

Going *to live abroad is exciting. It is also stressful.* The first year of living abroad is equal, in terms of stress, to several normal years at home and is a challenge for any family. For families faced with special challenges, such as stepfamilies, single-parent families, or families with members with special needs, the stress level is even higher. These families should consider a move abroad carefully. If they decide to go, they must find out what resources are available and consider how to cope with the challenges.

Some conditions are exacerbated by the stress of moving abroad— alcoholism, for instance, and some psychological conditions. Abroad, treatment options are often limited or inaccessible because of language and cultural differences. Occasionally the host country offers better treatment alternatives than those available at home. Discuss the situation with your doctor or therapist before leaving home, and get as much information as possible about the situation in the host country before making a decision.

The challenges facing one family member are challenges for all. This is true in any situation, but families are thrown together much more abroad than at home. When they arrive in the host country, they don't know anyone else and must depend on each other for company and support.

Stepfamilies

For stepfamilies, moving abroad is an added challenge. In a foreign place, family members are dependent on each other in a way that they are not at home. When they first arrive, siblings may be the only playmates. Parents rely on older children to help unpack and settle in or to watch out for younger siblings in new schools. However, going abroad is also an opportunity to weld a family together—"us" against the "outside world." At home, stepparenting situations are often complex. Children shuttle between families on weekends and must shift between different sets of family mores and demands. Abroad, children often spend semester time with one family and vacations with another, allowing more time for adjustment.

If at all possible, avoid moving abroad shortly after marriage. Give everyone time to settle down before making such a change. A situation in which a stepparent must raise the children because the natural parent is away much of the time is particularly difficult. Make sure that the natural parent is at home as much as possible, at least until the children have adjusted, or they may feel deserted. This is devastating for them and puts stepparents in a no-win situation.

Noncustodial parents at home are sometimes upset when children change while living abroad. They can react with alarm, particularly if children have picked up what they consider "foreign" ways. Encourage children to keep close contact with absent parents through e-mails, phone calls, and pictures. The more these parents understand their children's lives abroad, the less they will see expatriate life as a negative or insidious influence.

> Jane is putting enormous effort into raising her 15-year-old stepdaughter in Amman, Jordan, according to the principles laid down by her husband. Jane is not always in agreement with these, but her husband, who travels a great deal, phones constantly to check on his daughter. Jane and her stepdaughter argue constantly.

If a natural parent travels frequently, leaving a stepparent and children alone in a foreign country, establish guidelines for child-rearing and discipline. Traveling parents must trust and support the judgment of "home" partners. It simply doesn't work to leave partners with the responsibility for children's behavior but not give them the autonomy and authority to make decisions and carry them out. If children of both parents are living abroad, the children whose parent travels may feel disadvantaged. It is difficult for a stepparent in this situation to be fair, and even harder to be seen to be fair. One child I know went to boarding school rather than live with his stepmother and stepbrother.

In expatriate communities stepfamilies are not as common as at home. Other children may therefore be curious about the family situation. Talk openly with your children about their family. Answer their questions. This way they will know how to answer others. If necessary, remind teachers to include different family types in class discussions of family.

To protect stepfamilies:

- *Avoid overseas moves soon after marriage.* This is already a stressful time, and an overseas move can make the adjustment process too difficult, sometimes with long-term consequences.
- *If the natural parent travels often, establish child-rearing guidelines.* Ensure autonomy and support for the "home" parent.
- *Maintain regular contact with noncustodial parents in the home country.* Children change while they are abroad, and it is important that parents at home are given the opportunity to keep up with their development.
- *Prepare children to answer questions.*

Single Parents

I didn't set out to be a single parent abroad. My husband insisted that he would be willing to be the "trailing spouse" and look after Mara. But he couldn't find a job, and six months after we arrived in Lagos he left. I was devastated and felt so alone, but I was committed to an overseas career, so Mara and I have stayed abroad. Since then, though, I have applied for the safer postings because I can't always go places with her. We're fine now and we are a real team, but it was very hard at first.

Abroad, single parenting is particularly stressful. Many demands and problems come at once: settling in, finding your way around a new country, getting used to a new job, coping with children's problems. At home, single parents often have support from family or friends, or share childcare with the children's other parent. Abroad, they are really on their own, and single parents, particularly those going abroad for the first time, must have good coping skills to survive the settling-in period.

Some postings and situations are more viable for single parents than others. Talk to people who have lived in a place before accepting a job there. Consider your employer and the conditions. Are you expected to be up and running five seconds after you arrive, or will you have time to settle into the job and environment? Is good child care available? Is housing supplied? Single parents have limited time to deal with the mundane issues of apartment hunting, getting things fixed, organizing furniture, and so forth.

Build support systems as soon as possible. There are not many single parents in expatriate communities, but there are many spouses with traveling partners with whom you could develop mutual support networks. Many expatriate spouses are not employed and may be happy to take your child to ballet lessons or have her over to play. Of course, you will need to reciprocate, but you can often help in some other way. Many spouses feel isolated from the business world they used to be part of and may be grateful if you keep them up to date on what's happening or help them develop new skills.

To protect single-parent families:

- *Choose a posting where it is viable to combine work and parenting.*
- *Build a support network* of other parents, child-care providers, and other services.
- *Accept help* when it is offered.

Pseudo Single Parents

Heike lives in Argentina with her husband and two boys. Actually, Heike and the boys live in Buenos Aires while Wolfgang travels for seven months of the year. Although Heike found it a real struggle to begin with, she now has a group of friends with whom she can share child care and problems, and she is proud of her organizational skills. However, problems often arise when Wolfgang comes home. The daily routine changes and Wolfgang, feeling that the boys need a father's discipline, takes over. Heike welcomes his support but resents being pushed aside. After he leaves, it takes several days for the boys to settle down.

Many expatriate parents find themselves parenting alone while their spouses travel. Aside from the burden of raising children alone in a foreign environment, it is difficult to share responsibilities fairly when one parent comes and goes. Upon arriving home, some traveling spouses "take over," and at-home spouses may resent it. Or the traveling parent wants to relax when he gets home or only do fun things with the children. The at-home spouse wants some genuine help or time to relax herself.

To protect families in which the employee travels frequently:

- *Agree on general points of discipline* so that the traveling parent doesn't arrive home to, or with, a new set of rules.
- *Stick to a similar routine, whether the absent parent is there or not* (except for some fun times).
- *Share responsibilities, not just fun time.* Both spouses are entitled to some time in which to relax.
- *Schedule outings and family conferences* when the family is together.
- *Traveling spouses should keep up on what is happening at home* by telephone or e-mail so that parents can share decision-making responsibilities.

Divorce

When expatriates divorce, spouse and children must often return home because their rights of residence are dependent on the working partner. This adds a heavy load of stress to an already difficult situation. The spouse may have been unemployed for years and must make the transition back into the work force as well as reestablish a home and deal with reentry shock. She may not even be able to take the children with her. If she is not granted sole custody, she may not be able to leave the host country with the children. Country of residence is the basis for custody decisions, and she could be accused of kidnapping the children if she took them home without the spouse's permission. The European Union is trying to develop guidelines to alleviate this situation within these countries.

Courts in the country where you are resident generally have legal jurisdiction, and property division and financial support are subject to the laws of that country. In practice, courts often refer a couple back to their home country—where lack of residence can create problems! Not all countries have mutual agreements to enforce the decisions of other countries' courts. Agreements that give mothers custody, for instance, are not recognized in many Islamic countries. Many countries make little effort to enforce alimony and child support payments. Also, it is much easier for people working in the global economy to hide income—although recently introduced checks and balances make this increasingly difficult. Some employees hide behind diplomatic immunity. Even the United Nations only recently agreed to help ex-spouses collect child support payments from their employees. Organizations deal with the divorce situation in different ways. Some will pay the return expenses for spouse and children, while others consider this a private matter.

Accompanying spouses should know how much their partners earn and where money is banked or invested. Insist on transparency and joint authority over bank accounts and investments. Find out what the laws are of the host country are and how they are generally applied to foreigners. In the case of marital breakdown, look for a lawyer with expertise in applying private international law. Because this is a complex field, you will need good advice. Ask embassies or chambers of commerce for the names of lawyers. Muster all the social support you can gather abroad and at home because this is a difficult time and you will need support to help you through. Be prepared to call on professional counselors or mediators.

Gabby's mother called regularly, insisting that Gabby tell her when her father was next returning to Britain so that he could be arrested for missing child support payments. Gabby was confused and frightened. She had only recently gone to live with her father in Dubai and wanted to build a good relationship with him. On the other hand, she didn't want to let her mother down.

Children should not be drawn into their parents' battles, either at home or abroad. Fighting battles across international borders is immensely frustrating. When children are the only connection between parents separated by oceans and continents, it is tempting to use them as go-betweens. However, there are other ways to deal with these difficulties. Isolina Ricci,[*] for instance, suggests that partners move from an intimate to a business relationship. As in a business relationship, meetings should be by appointment, calls made only during business hours, and agreements made in writing. In the expatriate situation, consider how you would behave with an overseas business partner. Where and how would you organize meetings? What are the most effective means of communication? If it is difficult to call during business hours because of time differences, organize a mutually agreeable schedule. All agreements should be written and, as in cross-cultural situations, leave little room for misinterpretation.

To protect yourself and your children in the case of divorce abroad:

- *Insist on transparency in financial matters.* Spouses should know how much employees earn and where money is invested.
- *Find out how your organization deals with divorce.* Does your spouse's organizational status (e.g., diplomatic status) affect you?
- *Get information about host- and home-country laws.* Embassies often have this information or can recommend a source of information.

---

[*] Ricci, Isolina. *Mom's House, Dad's House: Making Shared Custody Work* (New York: Collier Books, 1982). This book includes a chapter on long-distance parenting that is useful for expatriates.

- *Use a lawyer with experience in international civil law.* Embassies may be able to recommend a lawyer. Ask other expatriates for referrals.
- *Avoid drawing children into marital battles.*

Family Violence

The stress of expatriate life can be a catalyst for violence-prone individuals. The absence of the recognized social norms of the home country can be disorienting and make it easier to justify lapses into violence. Sometimes there is less protection for spouses abroad. In some countries local authorities are reluctant to intervene when family violence involves foreigners; family disputes may be considered a private matter; it may be considered appropriate for men to physically "discipline" their wives; or the offender may have diplomatic status. Abroad, it can be difficult to leave a violent situation. Many countries have no system of safe houses for abused spouses, and language can make local resources inaccessible. With limited access to funds, it can be difficult to return home. Wives have been kept virtual prisoners by lack of funds for travel home or because they needed exit visas signed by their husbands to leave the country. Spouses of individuals with a history of abuse should consider a move abroad very carefully. Refuse to go to countries where marital abuse is considered "normal."

Children with Special Needs

Parents with special-needs children must consider how to cope abroad. There are large differences in the facilities available for children with disabilities as well as attitudes toward children with special needs. If children need special medical care, parents should get information about the availability of hospitals, clinics, specialists, and medications in the host country. Discuss with your doctors at home how various aspects of the new environment—climate, food, level of pollution, travel—could affect your child.

Michaelis, the 7-year-old son of Maria and Christos, is dependent on a wheelchair. Maria says, "It is really difficult a lot of the time. Even when there is a footpath, a lot of the time there are cars parked on it. And people don't even seem to know what the handicapped parking spaces are for. It is so frustrating, and I feel really bad when Michaelis can't go places because we physically can't get him there."

Attitudes toward physical and mental challenges vary. Not only do countries vary greatly in their provisions for people with disabilities, such as wheelchair-accessible buildings, but there are big differences in attitudes. These will affect children's sense of themselves, their ability to get around, and the amount of help they receive.

International schools cannot cope with children with significant special needs. Most of these schools do not have the facilities and staff to cater to children with significant physical, psychological, or mental difficulties. A few can provide help for children with mild to moderate learning problems, and schools will generally accept students with physical disabilities if their facilities are suitable. The facilities in local schools vary from one country to another.

To protect children with special needs:

- *Talk to doctors or therapists.* What impact could the move have? What treatment will be necessary in the future? What are the potential problems?
- *Get detailed information about available facilities.* What medical facilities are available? What facilities or programs are available for children with special needs?
- *Is schooling available for your child?* If your child cannot attend an international school, what alternatives are there?
- *Get information about cultural attitudes toward disabilities.* Contact doctors in the host country. Find out what facilities are available for people with disabilities. Are public buildings accessible to people with physical disabilities, for instance?

Adoption

British citizens, Alison and Tom are the happy parents of
two young boys from Sri Lanka. While living in Vienna,
they decided to adopt a baby girl from an orphanage in
Colombo. She had a cleft palate, but Alison, who comes
from a family of doctors, had already organized the necessary series of operations. As they were living in Austria, a
member of the European Union, British authorities insisted
that the necessary home study be done there. But when the
couple submitted the papers, the authorities in Sri Lanka—
who demanded a British or British-approved home study
because Alison and Tom are British citizens—rejected them.
Although British authorities accepted the Austrian home
study, they refused to endorse it because they had not com-
pleted it themselves. With time running out for the little
girl, who needed the operations as soon as possible if she
was to learn to talk, Alison and Tom asked that another
family adopt the child.

*Living abroad can simplify the adoption process in some cases and
complicate it in others.* Complex situations relating to citizenship and residence are a gray area that is not always covered
in legal formulations. There are also special issues involved
in traveling and living abroad with adopted children.

Sarah says, "At a hotel in Islamabad they tried to throw our
children out of the playground. The boys have dark skin
and, in their shorts and T-shirts, they thought the children
were beggars."

Each culture sees adoption in a different light. In some countries, adoption is seen as a noble thing to do. In others, it is
met with incomprehension, even hostility, particularly if the
children are racially different from their adoptive parents.
In some countries people will openly ask questions such as
"Are you the teacher?" or "Is your husband dark?" In others, they will stare or take sidelong glances. If your adopted

children are physically different from you, find out about attitudes toward adoption and racism before accepting a posting. What does the literature say about the racial situation in the host country? Contact international schools and ask about the experiences of students in that country. If possible, find other adoptive parents who are living there or have lived there.

> Lucy says, "When we arrived at Immigration, they said Tara had to join a different queue because she had a different passport. She's only 4 years old. We simply refused to let go of her, but it was really upsetting for all of us. I felt like going home again."

Travel on passports from the same country if at all possible. Many countries have different queues for different groups of people at immigration. Although few are absurd enough to insist that children stand on their own, it does happen. If your child can't yet take the same passport as you, have the adoption papers ready to show.

Children are sometimes curious and not always tactful, asking "Why are you a different color than your mother?" Talk openly with your children about such issues. Answer your children's questions simply and truthfully. This prepares them to answer the questions that other people ask. There is racism even in international schools. Although international schools have students from many countries and cultures and in many ways are an easier environment for children who are different, they are not free from racism. If there is a problem or incident, speak to teachers immediately.

> Alison says, "Rohan's third-grade teacher told me that she had asked all the children to tell the class where they were from. The other children said they were from Britain or Ghana or Taiwan and so on. When it was Rohan's turn, he launched into a long story about coming from Sri Lanka but that he had found a new Mommy and Daddy, so he also came from Britain and then he lived in Istanbul so he also came from

there. When it was the next child's turn she was at a bit of a loss. 'I'm just from Australia,' she said."

"Where are you from" is even more complicated for adopted expatriate children. Again, answer your children's questions openly and discuss all the places they are from. Help them feel that it is an advantage to have lots of places to be from, rather than feeling that they are not from anywhere.

To cope with adoption abroad:

- *Get information about host-country attitudes toward adoption.* Check the pertinent literature about the country. Ask international schools what their students have experienced. Talk to other adoptive parents in the country if possible.
- *Travel on the same passports if possible.*
- *Talk to your children openly about adoption and their national backgrounds.* Such discussions help children answer the questions that others ask of them.
- *Talk to teachers about racist incidents.* If your children are confronted by racist attitudes at school, talk to teachers.

Cross-cultural Families

Ten-year-old Lance says, "At home my father speaks Finnish and my mother often speaks Latvian, especially when she's mad. I have to speak English at school, and the language here is German. Some of the Austrian kids get angry with me because I say I don't want to learn German."

Cross-cultural families have two home cultures to maintain, and possibly two languages. Children are often faced with another language in the host country and possibly yet another at school. Some children can deal with three or four languages; others cannot. This can mean making some tough choices in terms of what language(s) to speak at home or what host-country language(s) to learn. The choice of school is critical. Children with two languages at home as well as another at school should not change their educational language as long as they are abroad. Do not insist that children learn more than basic survival vocabulary in the host country.

Children will need help from parents to grasp the essentials of their cultures. The less exposure children have to each culture, the less they will learn about it, so make sure you have plenty of books and videos from your home countries. Read your children stories; tell them about your childhood; celebrate your countries' special days. Take your children to their various homes for vacations and encourage them to get to know family members and their children.

Living abroad can also make life easier for cross-cultural couples. Many find it easier to reach compromises abroad because it is neutral ground. Most bicultural families must settle in one spouse's country, and that country's culture almost always dominates the family. This is the culture that children spend most time in. The family of the "home" spouse has more contact and more influence, and whenever there is a decision to be made, the environment supports the "home" person. Everyone nearby sees things the same way. Cross-cultural partners abroad escape much of this pressure, making it easier for the partners to find a middle way.

To help cross-cultural families:

- *Help your children learn about both their cultures.* Living abroad, children will get most of their information about their countries and cultures from their parents.
- *Do not insist on too many languages.* Not all children can deal with two languages at home and one at school, as well as various host-country languages.
- *Encourage your children to see bi- or multiculturalism as an advantage.*

Chapter 8
Those Who Care for Our Children

Galileo says, "Roberto went over to a friend's house to play and came back covered in white powder and with scratches on his arms. I asked him what he'd been doing and he said that he and Irfan had been playing on a building site next to Irfan's house. I called Irfan's mother and asked her if she knew where the boys had been. She said that they played there quite often and she'd told the boys to be careful."

Everything about child care is cultural. We bring up children so that they will think, act and believe according to our culture. This is not so much deliberate as simply passing on the things we learned. As a result, we take many of the things we do with children for granted. I tend to assume that children need positive reinforcement, for instance, but people in some cultures avoid praising children in case they become arrogant or overconfident, a highly undesirable trait. In other cultures, people believe that praise attracts the attention of malevolent gods. In some cases children are not named until they are several years old in order to avoid such unwanted attention.

At home, others often care for our children: grandparents, babysitters, child care providers. Abroad, we also entrust our children to others, but often they are from different cultures. They will automatically do things differently than we do and may not understand how we expect them to behave toward our children. When we give instructions, a lot gets lost in translation. Child care providers will therefore treat our children according to their own culture much of the time. Contact with child care providers from other cultures is a great opportunity for our children to learn about these cultures, but we must proceed with care.

Other Parents

Going to friends' homes is an important part of children's development. Playing at home is a different social experience from interactions at school, and children should experience a variety of social situations. When our children go to their friends' homes, we entrust them to other parents. At home, other prople don't bring up their children exactly the same way we bring up ours, but they tend to have many of the same values and beliefs that we do. Abroad, if children's friends are from other cultures, there may be differences on every level.

In general, this contact is an enriching experience for children, but there are important issues, such as safety. In the Western world we tend to believe that we are masters of our own destiny, that "God helps those who help themselves." As a result, we accept responsibility for children's safety and tend to have a lot of rules. In some cultures, events are considered to be governed by fate or the will of some higher power, and people do not believe that they can avoid accidents to the same extent. As a result, there are fewer rules regarding safety. People from these cultures are not less concerned for their children — or ours — but have different attitudes toward safety.

How far can you go in mandating your standards in other people's homes? If we allow our children to go to friends' homes, we must accept other people's ways of doing things — except in matters of safety. We have to live with *our* sense of responsibility, now and in the future. Maintain your standards of safety, within reason and as inoffensively as possible. If you are concerned about your children's safety, talk to their friends' parents. Express your fears. Don't imply that they are negligent. Say, "I like S. to wear a seatbelt because I have seen programs on TV about injuries that can be avoided" rather than, "You should make children wear seatbelts in the car." If this does not work, have the children play at your home.

> Katie really wanted to go to this girl's thirteenth birthday party and she said the parents were going to be there, but when I picked her up there were kids all over the place and no parent in sight. When I saw the mother a few days later, she said the party had been going well, so she left — and kids had to learn to manage themselves anyway.

There are different views on when children should become responsible for themselves. In some cultures, children who have reached puberty are considered adults. However, many of us consider maturation a slower process and believe that parents should set limits for young adolescents. Although we may negotiate those limits, we expect to enforce them. Because of these differences, there are a variety of rules among international teenagers, making their social life more complex and sometimes creating conflict with parents, as well as some practical problems. For example, if your child has a different curfew from her friend's, what happens when she sleeps over at the friend's home?

Discuss the things you expect your children to do even in friends' homes, from saying, "Thanks for having me" to sticking to curfews or wearing seatbelts. Be tolerant if other ways of doing things do not threaten your children's safety. Many things are harmless—occasionally drinking coffee at one place, for instance, or watching too much TV at another. Home remains the strongest influence, and experiencing other people's ways of doing things is a wonderful opportunity for learning about other cultures.

> I couldn't believe it. When I went to pick up Jonah, the boys were watching "brutallo," violence and sex films. They're only 9, for goodness sake. What were those parents thinking of?

Not all differences are cultural. There are negligent parents abroad just as there are at home, and some things you will not be able to tolerate. But avoid making children's friends responsible for their parents' decisions. Continue to welcome them in your home if you decide not to let your children go to theirs.

> Angela says, "I knew that children in this country are supposed to be seen and not heard. But when I went to this lady's house, she said she believed children should have learning opportunities and showed how she did activities with them, but every time I went to pick up my daughter early, she was in a playpen alone in a room. I stopped taking her there."

Each country has a system for babysitters who come in for the evening when you want to go out or with whom you can leave a child when you go out during the day. Sometimes schoolchildren earn money in this way, or there are mothers who are licensed to take extra children into their homes for payment. If you leave your children with someone from the host culture, find out how children are generally raised in that culture. Ask babysitters how they plan to react if your child cries for a long time, throws a tantrum, or won't go to bed.

To ensure children's safety in other people's homes:

- *Find out about other people's ways of dealing with children.*

The more you know about other ways of doing things, the more comfortable you will feel and the safer your child will be.

- *Exercise tolerance, but ensure your children's safety.* It is good for children to experience cultural differences, but not at the expense of their safety.
- *There are limits to tolerance.* Your primary concern is your children's well-being.

Household Employees

In some countries expatriate families can afford — and are expected — to hire household help. Having someone to take over household chores and help with child care is liberating. Being able to join a yoga class or share an uninterrupted meal with a spouse makes for more relaxed parents and good relationships, but although many nannies or babysitters are good to children, they cannot replace us.

Nannies and housemaids can take care of our children, but they cannot raise them. They will often be a kind and caring addition to our children's lives. But coming from a different culture, they have different ways of raising children and will not be able to achieve our child-rearing goals or prepare our children to function in our culture. In many cases they don't interact with children in ways that promote linguistic and cognitive development. Their employee status means that they often can't effectively set and enforce limits. They are also temporary. They may leave for personal reasons, and eventually, of course, we will leave them. With the exception of some diplomats, expatriates can't take their children's child care providers with them when they move. And no matter how caring, caregivers' interest and concern for our children will not equal our own. Contact with child care providers can enrich children's lives, but raising children is our job.

Spend as much time as possible with your children until they have settled down. When they are new in a country, children need

a parent rather than an unfamiliar caregiver, and they need
familiar routines. Even when they are settled, continue to
spend time at home. Don't accept every invitation you receive if it means being out every night. It is easy to get caught
up in a situation in which children are fed, bathed, and put
to bed by caregivers more often than not, but evening is often the most rewarding family time. It is a time to eat together and share what has happened during the day, to help
with homework and read bedtime stories. Let your children
know ahead of time when you will be out.

Training and Education

> Sarah had a broad smile and an infectious laugh, and the
> children loved her from the first day. She bathed and dressed
> them, but she rarely chatted with them and never joined in
> their games. She did not know how. Her own childhood
> had been spent caring for younger brothers and sisters.
> Eventually she learned some of the games and loved them,
> becoming so absorbed that she simply did not notice when
> the children wandered away to do something else.

*Many maids and nannies have no formal training and limited
schooling.* They are often expert at taking care of children's
physical needs but unable to provide the intellectual and cognitive input we consider necessary. Nannies in Congo, for instance, watch their young charges playing and call them back
if they wander away, but they rarely encourage, play, or chat
with their charges. In general, only long-time nannies develop
a relationship that enables them to cater to the emotional needs
of the children entrusted to them.

*If necessary, teach nannies or housemaids basic skills, especially
first aid.* Send them to a first aid course if one is available. We
often assume that everyone knows about bacteria and viruses
as the cause of infection, or the treatment for common diseases and mishaps, but this is not always the case. Ask a local
doctor what the common attitudes toward illness or treatment
of ailments are in your host country. In some countries, for
instance, people believe that taking many tablets at once will

cure an illness faster. Standards of hygiene in your host country may not be what you are used to. Particularly if your new child care provider has not worked for expatriates before, be sure to explain what you expect.

Cultural Differences

> I came home one day in Monrovia to find my son in bed, piled with covers. He had a fever of 104 degrees, and sweat was pouring down his face. To his nanny's horror, I undressed him and sponged him off with cold water. She literally wrung her hands at this treatment, sure that her young charge would die. The doctor we called explained that children with a fever are always wrapped up warmly in Liberia. She thought this treatment might have developed because fevers in West Africa most commonly mean malaria, which causes shivers and trembling, making the patient appear cold.

Child rearing is strongly influenced by culture. A child care provider from another country will do things quite differently than you do and may have different attitudes on almost everything, from safety and health to honesty and fair play. Insist that child care providers do things your way in important areas like safety or equal treatment of boys and girls. Explain what you expect of them and what your children are and are not allowed to do. Make as few rules as possible. It is easier to follow rules when there aren't too many of them, and this helps ensure that the caregiver's relationship with your children continues to be spontaneous. But be realistic. You might change a few behaviors, but you won't change basic attitudes. In five years our Sri Lankan housemaid only once admitted that our son had behaved badly. She was much more likely to cover for him.

Differences add richness and interest to children's lives. Child care providers are a valuable addition to children's lives. Learning new ways of doing things adds cognitive richness and variety to their lives. Every time we traveled from Monrovia to Switzerland, our nanny Sarah got up very early and spent hours braiding our daughter's hair so that she would be beautiful for her relatives. To this day our children enjoy the ritual of dressing up. Many of their attitudes toward family have developed in the family-oriented atmosphere of Africa and the Middle East. Not so positive was our battle for equal treatment for our daughter. In Saudi Arabia one houseboy completely ignored her and would not give her what she asked for, while lavishing attention on our son.

Discipline

If they are to set limits for our children, child care providers must have some authority. We have to support them, but should we allow them to discipline our children? I preferred that caregivers let me know if my children misbehaved rather than punishing them themselves. This had some disadvantages. Many caregivers hate to tell tales, and you become the bad guy: "Swarna doesn't mind if I do that, but Mom blows a gasket." Parents must set the guidelines that child care providers are to enforce. Children need consistency, and many expatriate children have several caregivers in the course of their lives abroad.

> Natalie says, "I really wish I hadn't left Piet with a nanny so much. I'm sure it had a negative effect on him. I think when we're not there, they [the nannies] put the kids down. They talk down to them and are tough, even mean. I'm sure it affected his self-esteem."

Child care providers will use the kind of discipline they use at home, so ask them how they discipline children: "What would you do if your son…?," "If your daughter doesn't want to do her homework, how would you get her to do it?" When a friend's daughter began having nightmares, she discovered that the nanny had been telling her frightening stories to get her to behave. Bribery is common: "If you stop writing on the wall you can have ice cream." Tell your child care provider how you want her to handle situations. Be specific. "If S. climbs on top of the cupboards again, please…" Repeat your instructions regularly—they may go against the cultural grain.

When Stephan was 14 years old, an accident put him in the hospital. His parents hastened to the hospital, where they were confronted not only with their son's broken leg but also with the news that he had second-stage syphilis. Horrified, they investigated and found that their son and his friends had been inviting prostitutes home, bribing household employees not to tell.

This is an extreme case, but it demonstrates the delicate balance of power between children and household employees. Children are in a vulnerable position vis-à-vis employees, but at the same time they are in a position to misuse the vulnerability of employees. From "I want more cookies or I'll tell my mother you were mean to me" to "Here's a dollar if you don't tell my parents what we've been doing," children can learn bad habits or even put themselves at risk. Sometimes child care providers treat children as an extension of their employer or a junior boss. Make it clear to your children and to caregivers that they are in charge, but also outline their responsibilities. Insist that your children treat their caregivers with respect.

Children should still take responsibility for household tasks. At your next posting you might not have household help. It is also important that children be able to look after themselves. Expect your children to pick up things they have left around the house and to tidy their own rooms. Make them responsible for a few chores around the house. Be reasonable. My son always had (unsolicited) help from our housemaid when he cleaned the car, but they seemed to enjoy themselves, spraying water around and giggling.

Saying Goodbye

When our children left Robertsfield Airport in Liberia on a misty morning in 1990, they said goodbye to their nanny, Sarah, as if they were going off on another vacation. We never returned. Sarah went back to her village and disappeared in a bloody civil war that lasted eight years. Our son refused to talk about her for several years. One day he

> started talking about the things they had done together. We
> talked about how Sarah had put on her best dress and slept
> in curlers so that she would look nice to go out and see
> them off. Our son was finally able to grieve for her.

Leaving child care providers can be heartbreaking for children. If
you have been lucky, they have had a good relationship with
your children, and leaving will be hard for everyone. It is
tempting to try to protect children from grief by not telling
them you are leaving until the last minute or not telling them
that their caregiver won't be going with you. But your child
will grieve anyway. Not having a chance to say goodbye robs
children of the opportunity to take leave and express grief —
and to realize that their caregivers are also sad. The last hugs
and tears are important precursors to healing.

Chapter 9
Health and Safety

Therese says, "We took Simone to the emergency room. She was bleeding badly and screaming but no one reacted, or at least not what I would call react. They were so slow. Eventually they put eighteen stitches in her leg—pretty competently, and everything was clean—but I'm really glad she wasn't hurt worse. Later our family doctor said we should have called him. He would have organized everything."

In terms of health and safety, each country is a new situation. The health system will probably be very different from what we are used to. In some countries, you can just turn up at the hospital. In others, you must be brought in by ambulance or have a doctor's referral. You may be expected to prove that you have insurance before you receive treatment, or, as foreigners, to pay up front. Attitudes toward health and illness vary. While every life is fought for tenaciously in some places, death is considered unavoidable in others, a critical difference when a child's life is on the line. In each country there are different dangers. A new country may be safer than home in some ways and more dangerous in others. We need information about the hazards in a new country and about its health care system in order to protect our children.

Health

Moving is stressful, and so is the adjustment to a new environment and climate, posing a challenge to the immune system. The first steps to staying healthy in a foreign country begin before we leave. Stick to a healthy diet in the weeks before you leave. Take time off to relax. The whole family should go for a medical checkup, update immunizations if necessary, and get additional immunizations for the host country, if necessary.

Get as much information as possible before you leave. If you are going to a tropical region, visit a specialist or a tropical clinic and get expert advice on the best way to prevent and deal with illnesses in these areas. Find out all you can about the health care system in the new country. If it is inadequate, look for the fastest means of medical evacuation from the country and get the appropriate insurance coverage.

In the first few months many children often get ill regularly. Schoolchildren in particular pick up everything that is going around. In another country, the viruses and bacteria are likely to be different enough to outmaneuver your immune system. Take remedies for simple illnesses with you.

To prepare for going abroad:

- *Check conditions in the new country.* What are the dangers? Is the water safe to drink? Do fruit and vegetables need to be sterilized?
- *Find out about the health care system.* If it is inadequate, get information about medical evacuation and get appropriate insurance.

- *Have a medical checkup.* This should be repeated every
  year, especially if you will live in tropical areas or third
  world countries.
- *Find out if medications you might need are available.* If not,
  take them with you, but check host country regulations
  on their import first. Take simple remedies with you, as
  children often get ill in the first few weeks.
- *Take a few favorite foods with you, if possible.* Children
  often reject new foods at first, making it difficult to
  offer a balanced diet.

When You Arrive

Find out about health care services. Ask other expatriates and
local doctors. What hospitals and clinics are available? How
do you get there? Find a family physician as soon as possible.
Prevention is definitely better than cure, given the inadequate
health care services in many countries. Take as much action
as possible to prevent illness. Encourage a healthy diet. In countries with a limited range of foods, this calls for creative thinking. Ask other expatriates where they buy food items and for
recipes using new types of fruit and vegetables.

*Even in third world countries you can create a healthy environ-
ment.* Check the hygiene practices of household personnel,
particularly in the kitchen. See that household employees
have regular medical checkups, and provide medical care
for them. Pets should also have all the necessary inoculations.

To protect children's health in the host country:

- *Find out about health care services.* Ask other expatriates
  to recommend a family doctor. Practice getting to the
  nearest clinic. Teach children emergency telephone
  numbers and how to give your address in the local
  language.
- *Stick to a healthy diet, especially in the first few weeks.*
  Stress and travel create special needs. Add a good
  multivitamin to children's diet.
- *Develop good hygiene routines, especially in third world
  countries.* Make sure children wash their hands before

eating and carry wipes when traveling. Household help may have different ideas of hygiene, so observe how they work.

- *Household help should also have regular medical checkups.*
- *Pets should be inoculated and dewormed regularly.*

Mental Health

We don't leave our weaknesses behind when we fly to foreign shores. They are securely packed in the luggage of our psyche. We simply begin a new journey.

Change is not as good as a rest. Moving abroad is stressful, with elements that can trigger a variety of psychological conditions. Stress, disorientation, and periods of depression are part of the agenda for all expatriates but can overwhelm those who are already facing psychological challenges. If a member of your family has a history of psychological problems, consider an overseas move carefully. Some psychological conditions are permanent; others may recur under certain conditions. Some conditions, such as certain types of depression, neurosis, schizophrenia, or psychosis, have genetic components and the children of parents (or close family members) suffering from these illnesses may have a higher biochemical vulnerability to these illnesses. If these conditions have occurred in your family, seek professional advice. Consider ways to reduce stress abroad and look for treatment options in the host country as soon as possible.

A move is often viable only if adequate and appropriate support can be identified. Accept only postings with adequate treatment facilities, such as therapists who speak your language. Concepts of psychological health and illness are different in each culture, and finding appropriate treatment abroad can be difficult. Local facilities are often inaccessible because of language barriers. Although competent counselors can be found in most expatriate communities, psychiatrists are rare—a problem for those who need medication.

Four months after we arrived in Brussels, Aileen stopped eating. She said it all tasted horrible. I had suspected she was anorexic for months, but I didn't know how to talk to her about it. In Brussels we had a terrible time finding someone to treat her. I hardly knew anyone, and it was hard finding someone who spoke English well and whom Aileen felt comfortable with. Eventually she had to be admitted to a hospital. They were nice there and tried to speak English to her, but for the most part everyone spoke Flemish or French. When she was released I took her home.

Confront problems openly. If a family member has a problem, talk to a doctor, psychologist, or therapist at home before accepting a posting abroad. The repercussions of mental illness are more serious abroad. Treatment can be difficult to find, and an illness can mean that the whole family has to pack up and go home.

Be open with schools about children's problems. It is possible that they will refuse to accept children with severe psychological problems, but this is better than accepting them and then asking them to leave several months later. If this happens, the whole family may have to return home if another school cannot be found, and the child goes through a lot of disruption and experiences yet another failure.

Anna had a history of psychosis and had been under treatment for years when she and her husband and two young girls moved to Rome. Anna joined clubs and made friends. Her friends sometimes knew that she had bouts of depression but did not recognize the extent of her problems. Nor did anyone realize that Anna, more and more distressed, had begun taking high levels of medication without supervision. One night, two years after her arrival in Rome, Anna threw herself in front of a train.

The expatriate community has difficulty providing support for people with serious problems. In foreign countries other expatriates can provide only limited support. They have limited support themselves and are unfamiliar with emergency services. Friends are often too new to provide the kind of support needed or to know when a person is in real trouble. When people are not aware of a person's background, they are more likely to label those who behave differently as antisocial or difficult, thus further isolating them.

Finding Competent Professionals

Abroad, finding treatment for psychological problems is challenging. Language and cultural differences can make it difficult to use therapists from the host community, particularly for children. Communication problems make them feel uncomfortable or even threatened. If you use a local therapist, be aware of cultural differences in attitudes toward mental health and treatment. Meet a therapist before your child starts treatment. Try to find others who have used the therapist in question. Go by your instincts. Don't trust therapists just because they are "experts."

To find suitable therapists, ask around. Other expatriates may be able to recommend someone. Embassies may have lists of professionals who speak your language, possibly even fellow nationals who have settled in the host country. Ask school counselors for names. Trained counselors, psychotherapists, or psychologists may be available in the expatriate community. Some may not be locally licensed or may not have a work permit and therefore keep a low profile. Check that they are licensed in their country of origin.

If a member of the family has psychological problems:
- *Discuss the problem with a doctor or therapist at home.* Find out what kind of treatment will probably be needed in the future. Organize medication, if necessary, and appropriate supervision.
- *Check the resources available in the host country.* Ask doctors for referrals of colleagues working in the host country.
- *Build up a support network as soon as possible.* Locate

suitable professionals. Join interest groups and international groups.

Depression

Symptoms of depression can resemble those of culture shock. Many of the elements that are thought to cause depression are present in a move abroad. Depression can also be a forerunner of other problems. It is, therefore, the most important mental disorder for most expatriate parents.

> Ron and Maeve knew that their 15-year-old son, Sean, was not happy in Hamburg, but they thought he was still adjusting. He hadn't really made friends, and he had lost interest in schoolwork, even though he had always been a reasonable student. He spent most of his time in his room. One night, after an argument, Sean ran out of the house without a jacket, money, or house key. He did not come back. Since there were no friends or family members he could go to, his parents spent a fearful night searching the city. When Sean turned up in the morning, they knew it was time to look for help.

Expatriate parents should be on the lookout for depression in their children. Many factors thought to contribute to depression are part of moving abroad: loss, stress, loneliness, communication and school problems. Children who suffer significant losses are more prone to depression. Many expatriate children experience losses of caregivers, friends, pets, and familiar environments. Many also experience lengthy separations from one parent because that parent travels frequently. Being the new kid in school almost always means a period of loneliness, especially for children who must change their educational language. A school day is very long for a child who can neither speak to nor understand others.

Severe depression is not to be taken lightly. A significant percentage of people with serious depression commit suicide, adults and children alike. Children who write or talk about death or suicide must be taken very seriously.

Detecting Depression

How do we know if children are depressed? They can't put a name to what is wrong and do not always act depressed. Some get involved in everything, covering up their misery with a whirl-wind of activity. Many of the behaviors we associate with depression are also reactions to moving. Changes in eating or sleeping patterns can result from changes in the child's environment. Anger and sadness are typical reactions to frustration and loneliness. And children moving abroad sometimes feel depressed, but *feeling* depressed and *being* depressed are not the same thing. One is a normal, transient phase that passes relatively quickly; children feel depressed for a while but soon cheer up and get on with their lives. True depression is a constant state of mind that overwhelms children, stopping them from enjoying the things they usually do. So how do we differentiate between "normal" responses to a move and real depression?

Detecting depression in children is difficult, especially during a move. Serious depression should be diagnosed by a professional. However, parents usually notice changes in their children. Younger children often act up more. They throw tantrums more often or have screaming fits. Older children may start acting differently in some way. Many parents recognize that something is wrong with their child but can't quite put their finger on it. Trust your instincts. If you feel worried, consult a doctor or therapist.

Pay attention to how long moods or periods of unusual behavior last. Is a child upset or sad for a day or so at a time, for instance, or has the depressed or angry mood lasted several weeks? Therapists recommend keeping a diary because parents tend to underestimate the severity or duration of symptoms.

Teachers may also detect problems. They spend a lot of time with their students and can compare a student with others.

Listen carefully if teachers express concern. If you stick to similar routines in the new country, it is easier to tell whether your children's behaviors have changed. Be available to children during the transition phase, to provide extra support and also to keep an eye on how things are developing.

Symptoms of depression:

- *Lack of interest in things that used to be important.* Usual activities may not be available, and it can take some time to find others. But pay attention if a child loses interest in everything.
- *Tiredness and lack of energy.* All active children get tired, but children who have been hanging around shouldn't be tired without something major, such as a climate change, to account for it.
- *Lack of concentration.* You ask children to do something but they don't remember to do it. Lack of concentration also affects classroom behavior, and teachers are sometimes the first to detect problems.
- *Changes in sleep habits.* If there is nothing connected with the move to account for changes in sleep habits, such as getting used to traffic noise or air-conditioning, pay attention if a child sleeps a lot more than usual, cannot sleep, or is constantly tired.
- *Changes in appetite.* Depressed children may comfort themselves with food or avoid food altogether, even their favorite foods. However, "I'm not hungry" or "This tastes funny" may be reactions to climate changes or new foods.
- *Physical complaints.* A child may complain of feeling ill with no obvious cause and want to stay home from school. Check with teachers to make sure there are no classroom difficulties that could be making the child reluctant to go to school.
- *Negative self-image.* Depressed children constantly put themselves down or talk about being unloved and worthless. They are unable to acknowledge successes.
- *Aggressive behavior.* Children may pick fights with parents or siblings or engage in destructive behaviors. This is also a common reaction to the frustrations of a

new environment, but there are differences between frustration and misery.
- *Hyperactivity.* Some depressed children are hyperactive, running away from pain or depression by keeping on the move.
- *Fearfulness or unusual risk taking.* In new environments children are often afraid of or, alternatively, underestimate new dangers. In contrast, depressed children tend to be fearful even in familiar situations or may suddenly take deliberate risks.
- **Talk of death or suicide.** If a child writes or talks about death or suicide, take action immediately.

Dealing With Depression

The first step is to consult a doctor. Sometimes children show symptoms of depression because they have a physical illness. If this turns out not to be the case, consult a psychologist or psychotherapist. Let the school counselor know that your child has a problem. Children may find it easier to talk to someone outside the family.

Get information about depression. Talk to your children, the one who is depressed as well as his or her siblings. Help them understand what depression is and that the depressed person cannot help it. Emphasize that depression can be treated, but be realistic; healing takes time even after treatment begins. Keep lines of communication open. Depressed children may not talk much, but listen carefully when they do. Make sure they still participate in family time such as mealtimes, but keep communication simple, as depressed children often have trouble concentrating. Encourage participation in social events of any kind to avoid isolation.

> Rhonda says, "When we first went to Mailand, Amy seemed really down. She didn't have anyone to go out with on weekends or she just couldn't organize things, so we planned family outings every weekend. It seemed to do her good, and although we would sometimes have rather stayed

home, we enjoyed having time with her. Eventually she made friends and started to go out with them."

Activity is a natural pick-me-up. Get children out and moving. Any activity is good, particularly physical activities. Depressed children often have trouble getting organized, so let them know ahead of time when they are expected to be ready. Spending time around someone who is depressed is, literally, depressing. Find time for yourself. Encourage siblings to support the depressed child but to continue their normal activities.

If your child is depressed:

- *Consult a doctor.* Make sure the child does not have a physical illness.
- *Get information about depression.* Help the child and his or her siblings understand what it is.
- *Avoid isolation.* Keep your children involved in family events. Encourage them to participate in other social activities.
- *Encourage sports and fun activities for the whole family.* Siblings should continue their normal activities, and parents should seek some relaxation.

Avoiding Depression

Moving can *contribute to depression, but it doesn't have to.* When we move children from a country where they can manage much of their daily lives to one that is completely different, they often feel that they have lost control. It is therefore important to let them make age-appropriate decisions and to help them master the new environment.

Children should be challenged but not overwhelmed. It's a bit of a balancing act to let children handle as much of their environment as possible but not be overwhelmed by it. Be available to your children during the adjustment phase. Make time for a chat or to play a game or do an activity, or drive them somewhere. Talking and listening to children helps in judging how they are doing. It gives us the opportunity to provide support at the right moment. Games and activities help children keep stress levels down so that they are better able to deal with any problems that do arise.

To prevent depression in children:

- *Give children some control over their lives.* Let them participate in some decisions; encourage them to master the new environment and solve their own problems.
- *Communicate.* Be available, especially during the adjustment period. Keep in touch with your children.
- *Reduce stress levels.* Choose schools carefully, provide support, and encourage fun activities.

Safety

> Fernanda says, "I was scared living ten stories up, but I kept telling myself that everything would be fine. Then there was a fire in the building. It wasn't serious, but we didn't even know what was happening because there were no smoke alarms. Our lawyer said that legally there should be, so we insisted they be installed."

Abroad, safety often rests in parents' hands. We must find out what the new dangers are and how to use emergency facilities. This is a heavy responsibility, and to make it worse, we sometimes perceive things as more dangerous because we are nervous in a foreign country. The best antidote is reliable and detailed information. It is not enough to know that there are dangerous snakes in your host country, for instance. Find out how common they are where you are living, what they look like, how to react if you do see them, and which clinics keep antidotes. That way you will not worry about something that, perhaps, is never seen in your area, and if you are confronted with a dangerous situation you will know how to deal with it.

Insist on children's compliance on safety issues. We are often tempted to adapt to the local safety norms, which may be more relaxed than those we are used to. But safety is important, especially in countries where health care is not optimal. Seatbelts and bicycle helmets should be worn no matter where you are living. Learning about traffic safety is important everywhere. Children will often conform if friends do the same, so have an extra helmet available for children who come to your home to play with your children.

Feeling Secure

Children need not only to be safe but also to feel *safe.* These are not always the same thing. Children experience the world differently than adults and have different ideas about what is threatening. Be sensitive to what makes your children feel afraid. Discuss their fears. Even subjective fears and anxieties should be taken seriously. Don't give children the feeling that their concerns are silly or babyish. Be equally sensitive to the things that make them feel safe. If they want you to close the curtains, leave a light on at night, or check under the bed to make sure there are no monsters there, oblige them. Parents are able to give children a feeling of security, so stay calm and positive.

Legal issues

> The drug situation in Cyprus was easy in some ways. Although some of the kids at the school smoked marijuana, it was easy to persuade our son not to. He really wanted to pass his exams, and he couldn't do that if he was caught and thrown out of the country.

Even though they are foreigners, expatriates are still subject to the laws of the host country. Teenagers and their parents in particular need to be aware of the laws and some of the moral codes. In Holland, for example, marijuana can be sold legally. In other countries possession of drugs, even marijuana, is a very serious offence carrying heavy penalties and in some cases the death sentence. Other countries expel young foreigners for minor drug infringements. In most Western countries penalties are lower for children below the legal age of consent, but in some countries even teenagers must take full responsibility for their actions.

It can also work the other way around. In the United States, Australia, and New Zealand, young people are not served alcohol, and teenagers coming from one of these countries often are not prepared to cope with the ready availability of alcohol in other countries. In Europe, 16-year-olds can go to bars, which are often meeting places for youngsters. In other countries, although the drinking age is higher, it is not always enforced.

Host country legal systems may not protect your children as they did at home. Wearing seatbelts in cars may not be mandatory, for instance, or the laws are not enforced. Lack of consumer protection or hygiene regulations may also increase the number of unsafe products available. Even going to a fun fair can be a more hazardous outing abroad than at home. Without overreacting, be prepared to protect children when the law does not. Insist that they put on their seatbelts, wear bicycle helmets or protection while roller-blading, and not buy food from roadside stalls. Be realistic. Children are not always obedient. If you want to prevent them from buying certain foods, provide attractive alternatives.

Moral Issues

One balmy evening in New Delhi, while dropping off her son David's Indian girlfriend, Ruth watched the young couple kiss on the doorstep of the apartment block. "You should at least go inside," she said. "Anyone seeing Vedana kissing might jump to the wrong conclusion. Unmarried girls aren't supposed to go out alone with men here, let alone kiss in public." David was upset with his mother, but the next day at school Vedana admitted that her mother was also upset, especially because the two women lived on their own.

Host country mores affect our children. Dress is important because it is often the first thing people notice about a person. In Saudi Arabia and Iran, girls are legally required to dress in a certain way. In North America, Europe, or Australasia, scanty clothing does not, in general, indicate that a girl is looking for sexual encounters. In other countries this may be precisely the message it sends. Being familiar with host country customs makes for greater safety.

Fitting in helps children feel at home. When children break the host country's cultural rules, people react negatively, even angrily. Help your children avoid such situations. If you notice them doing something that offends, call their attention to it. Congratulate them when they get it right. Make a game of finding out how local people do things. Recount your own experiences and set a good example. However, don't put too much pressure on your children in this regard. Many children like to find their own compromises and balances, or they simply need time to adjust.

Travel Safety

Expatriate children travel. Prepare them to deal with emergencies. Start early with simple instructions. Make a game out of it if possible: "Who will be the first to find the hotel fire exit?" "Does anyone know how to call reception?" "How many rows are there to the next exit?" "Who knows where the life vests are?" Children should develop the confidence that they can survive if they do the right things. Studies show that people who think about how to deal with crises have a higher survival rate. However, if your child is sensitive or has a very active imagination, take it slowly and gently. Underplay the dangers without skipping essential information.

To ensure your children's safety:

- *Make safety a primary consideration.* Insist on safe housing. Choose a car for its safety features. Check safety procedures at school.
- *Get reliable information.* What crimes are prevalent?

What parts of the city should you avoid? Talk to
expatriates as well as local people. If you are very
lucky, your organization provides access to good safety
information or to a safety specialist.

- *Get information on host country laws and mores.* Discuss
these with your children. When laws give your children more freedom than they are used to, decide what
is reasonable and safe.

- *Insist on children's compliance on safety measures.*
Seatbelts and bicycle helmets should be worn no
matter where you are living.

- *Plan for emergencies.* What are the numbers for emergency services? How can you get to the nearest hospital? Make sure your children know emergency
numbers and can call you if there is trouble. Have
mobile phones if possible.

- *Teach appropriate responses to new dangers.* Practice those
responses regularly. Keep them simple and be calm.

- *Help your children **feel** safe.* Take their fears seriously
even if they are not rational. Be sensitive to what
makes your children *feel* safe.

Chapter 10
Developmental Stages

George was only 6 years old when he left Brazzaville and does not remember much about the five years he spent there, but the country and culture have left traces. Some of them he is aware of: "I hate heavy clothing or tight things. I never wear jeans." His father, however, thinks that living in Congo influenced him in other ways. "George makes friends with everyone. He doesn't care where they come from. His wife is actually from Senegal," he says. "And George just has attitudes that he didn't get from me. He doesn't take things as seriously as I do. He's always telling me to 'lighten up' or something like that."

The effects of moving and living abroad depend on the child's age. Living abroad has a profound impact on young children. This is a period of rapid development and children are "pro-grammed" in many ways by their environment, which in the case of expatriate children includes a host country. As adults we interpret the foreign environment in the light of cultural programing learned at home, but young children do not yet have such filters in place. They soak up what is around them more or less indiscriminately. Because young children learn by imitating, they mimic the behaviors of the people around them. Adolescents going abroad for the first time are not affected in the same way. Their minds are already programmed to some extent. They are more inhibited by language and cultural differences and usually don't throw themselves into the host country culture or the expatriate community in the same way. On the other hand, they consciously reflect on their experiences. Having other-culture friends helps them develop the ability to consider other people's perspectives. In general, living abroad broadens their horizons. The majority will maintain an interest in international affairs throughout their lives.

Infants (0–2 years)

Infants develop rapidly from helpless babies to relatively coordinated 2-year-olds. During this time the physical, cognitive, and emotional foundations are established, but infants are not passive spectators in the process. They actively investigate their world, finding out how they can make things happen—for example, moving a hanging toy or smiling at someone and getting a smile in return. In this way they learn what is predictable and develop rules about how the world works. When we take them to a new country, they continue this process, developing yet another set of rules for the new environment. For example, while their parents allow them to crawl in the garden, the nanny picks them up and carries them around.

Children cannot make sense of information that changes too often. A complex environment helps infants develop a rich subjective world and may stimulate cognitive development. If it changes too much and too often, however, they may give up trying to make sense of it. Infants need a core of consistent conditions. Fortunately, even when moving, parents can provide a relatively stable environment. Stick to similar routines. Maintain consistent rules. If you read stories to your toddler at bedtime at home, continue to do so in the new country.

Infants are adaptable, accepting rather than questioning their environment. They learn primarily by watching and imitating the people around them—not just parents but caregivers and other children as well. If you leave your children with a nanny, for instance, the nanny's culture will determine how she behaves toward them and what they learn from her. Cultural differences in childrearing begin at birth, from whether mothers respond to babies' cries or ignore them to whether toddlers are encouraged to be dependent or independent. If you are going to leave your children with a child care provider, find out how people in the host culture generally raise children.

Relationships

Children's relationships to parents affect their other social relationships. Children who feel secure and loved are more curious, relate better to adults and other children, and are more confident. When you move to a new country, don't endanger your relationship to your children or their feelings of security by suddenly handing them over to a nanny. Give them time to get used to the new environment and get to know the nanny before leaving them alone with her. And do not give up your role as the main person in your children's lives. Expatriate children in particular need stable figures in their lives, and only you can pass on your own cultural mores.

Reactions to strangers and new child care providers depend on age. At the age of six to seven months, infants start rejecting strangers, a response that increases until around fifteen months. Later most children become open and friendly with other people, at least in situations in which they feel secure.

Transitions

Flying with babies up to the age of about nine months is relatively easy. They don't move around too much and can sleep in aircraft baby baskets. Traveling with toddlers is strenuous. They often hate to sit still and wander off in crowded airports or want to toddle around planes, where drinks and food trays are at just the right height to grab. Prepare for flights carefully with a few snacks and some entertainment. Travel with your spouse when possible.

Infants respond quickly and emphatically to new places. A few children placidly take everything in their stride, but most respond with distress to changes in their environment. They may take a temporary step backward in development, wetting the bed again, clinging to parents, or crawling instead of walking, but they will catch up again when they settle down. In the meantime, provide as much reassurance and comfort as you can. We can control many of the things infants don't like, such as changes in routines, food, or play, so stick to normal routines. Take some familiar foods with you. Pack your children's favorite toys. Don't worry that your children will not learn to cope with change. There is plenty of time for new things after they are settled.

Infants can become very ill very quickly, even from simple illnesses. Getting information about diseases and hazards in your new country is a priority. Find out what health care services are available and how to get to clinics and hospitals. Check the hygiene habits of house personnel.

Even infants can respond with intense grief to the loss of child care providers when you have to leave a posting. This grief is intensified because in the mind of an infant when people disappear they cease to exist. Toddlers should be given the opportunity to bid farewell to caregivers, even for temporary absences such as vacations. Give them extra attention and reassurance during these phases.

To help infants:

- *Provide security and stability.* Stick to routines and familiar foods during the first weeks.
- *Provide additional comfort.* Hug your children more often. Comfort and reassure them when they are upset.
- *Introduce child care providers slowly.* Consider cultural

differences and developmental age. Children between 6 and 15 months may take longer to get used to caregivers.
- *Get information about medical services as soon as possible.* Small children can get very ill very quickly.

Early Childhood (3–5 years)

This is also a period of exploration in which children add to their knowledge of the world and their own place in it. However, for developmental reasons their perceptions are not always accurate. Unable to differentiate reliably between cause and effect, a child may believe, for instance, that graveyards *cause* death because they have dead people in them. Differentiating between appearance and reality also causes difficulty. Children may think that wearing a mask at Halloween or Carnival changes the person wearing it. Children of this age are intensely egocentric and often misinterpret their place in the world, thinking that they have caused things to happen when this is not the case. The loss of a child care provider may be perceived to be a result of their misbehavior, for instance. Children's behavior also reflects inaccurate perceptions. In a new environment children may develop fears that have no obvious cause. Take these fears seriously and offer reassurance: "I know you are really scared that there are snakes in the room. Abdullah told me that he has never seen any snakes in the compound, but would you like me to make sure? Then I'll stay with you for a little while until you go to sleep again."

Children readily learn different social patterns, but they become confused in unfamiliar situations. When they don't understand the rules, they may invent something or make illogical associations, such as "Our houseboy doesn't eat with us because his daddy won't let him." Help children understand the new social patterns around them and how they are expected to behave. Children can now conceive of things or people that are not present and know that grandparents, for instance, have not disappeared because they aren't there.

Reinforce this awareness by hanging up pictures of absent family members or friends, or give your children photo albums. Ask their grandparents to keep in touch.

Relationships

Child care providers will influence children. Adults shape young children's reality by communicating their own perceptions of the world and by modeling the way to do things. Young children also believe what they are told. They are only just learning to differentiate between truth and fiction. In some cultures, frightening stories are used to control children: "There is a big black spider that comes to get children who don't go to bed when they are told." If you are employing caregivers from another culture, find out how they discipline children.

A friend, at this age, is someone to play with. Children often play with whomever lives nearby, so look for a neighborhood with other children. Culture and language differences often are no hindrance. Young children tend to talk "at" each other rather than engaging in dialogue anyway, and this contact provides a great opportunity for children to learn language skills and how to get along with children from other cultures. If your children are going to friends' homes without you, find out how the parents deal with safety issues. If you cannot agree with things your children's friends are allowed to do, invite the friends to play at your home instead.

Preschools

Many expatriate parents send children to local preschools. Academic issues are not yet important, and there may be a preschool close to home. However, there will be cultural differences, so check that the school is what you want for your children. In good schools parents are welcome to look around and observe sessions. If a different language is spoken, make sure children have a survival vocabulary, such as how to ask to go to the toilet. If not, ask if you can stay with them at school for a week or two.

Preschools should provide:

- *A program of suitable activities* that promote intellectual, social, emotional, and physical development.
- *Child care providers with specialized training.*
- *A low child-teacher ratio.*
- *A safe environment.*

Transitions

Explain a move to children. They like the important things in life to be predictable, so avoid unwelcome surprises. Tell them what is planned. Also prepare them for the new place. Will the weather be warm or cold? Can you move straight into a home or will you stay in a hotel? Will your possessions already be there? To help them feel more secure, let them choose a "transition object"—for example, a small toy or a security blanket—to be packed in the luggage you take with you. Young children often can't tell you why they are upset or what they are feeling, but be ready with comfort and reassurance.

Children form strong attachments to child care providers. When you leave a country and a nanny must be left behind, help children find ways to say goodbye—by giving a gift or photo, for instance. Acknowledge that it is sad to leave behind people you care about. Children may also be angry because they are losing someone they love and they can't do anything about it. Never leave without telling your children that the child care provider is not coming with you. Children can become afraid that other important people could also disappear from their lives without warning.

To help young children:

- *Explain about moving.* Make a move as predictable as possible by explaining what will happen and when.
- *Look for a neighborhood with children.*
- *Provide security and stability.* Stick to familiar routines and foods for the first few weeks.
- *Provide additional comfort.* Hug your children more

often; comfort and reassure them when they are upset.
- *Expect regressive behavior and don't overreact.* Children may take a step backward in development, but this is usually temporary.
- *Check important childrearing attitudes of child care providers.*
- *Check preschools carefully.*

Middle Childhood (6–12 Years)

Schoolchildren spend much of their time with people outside the family, particularly teachers and friends. For expatriate children this often means spending a lot of time with people from other cultures. They will be confronted with different sets of rules, particularly social and moral rules. Young schoolchildren like to follow rules exactly and are sometimes confused by the different sets of rules they encounter at home and school. They will insist, "But my teacher says you always have to say 'please' and 'thank-you'" even if for linguistic or cultural reasons this is not usual at home.

Preadolescence brings many changes, including puberty, for many children. As children slowly become socially and intellectually independent, they no longer believe everything parents say and begin to challenge their parents' positions on many issues. Although they are now capable of reasoning, this skill is not well developed and they have difficulty engaging in rational discussions. As a result, this can be a time of less positive interactions between parents and children. However, family is very important for preadolescents, so it is worth taking the time to work out problems and grievances, no matter how silly they may seem. This is the time when a working relationship that will continue into adolescence is established.

Relationships

Friendships are no longer based simply on joint activities; instead, they are based on shared interests and involve understanding and trust. Rather than playing with children in the neighborhood, children now want to go and play at friends' homes. As friends are often made at school, living near the school, where school friends are also likely to live, can save parents a lot of driving. It also makes it easier for children to participate in school activities.

> When Sylvia and Laurence moved to Zaire, their three children attended an American international school for the first time. Jessica, 11 years old, was caught up in the pressure to "be American" — and so was her mother. Overnight, her daughter wanted to change her whole wardrobe and shave her legs, something unheard of for a child in her own country.

Belonging and being socially accepted become increasingly important, especially in the years just before puberty. Although expatriate children, especially if they are in international schools, get used to an environment in which everyone is different, they still have moments of wanting to be the same, of wanting the same T-shirts or shoes as their friends. Newcomers now find it more difficult to become accepted. Because more is shared in friendships, trust becomes an issue and children prefer friends whom they know well. If children are abroad for the first time, they may have difficulty bridging cultural differences to make friends. Many first make friends with students from their own country. Encourage them to also look further, as they may have more in common in terms of interests and abilities with children from other cultures. Joining activity groups can help them find like-minded friends.

> Anita says, "There were only four girls in my class, and none of them wanted to be friends with me so I started playing with the boys. The other girls were nasty about it, but at least I got to play with somebody."

Schoolchildren of this age prefer to be with others of the same sex. This affects children at international schools because it halves the number of potential friends in schools that are already small. If your children have trouble finding friends, encourage them to look outside their school, perhaps in other international schools if there is a language barrier to the host community, or in activity groups of some kind.

School

The younger children are, the easier it is to change schools, but getting used to a new school is never easy, and schools abroad are likely to be quite different from those at home. Expect children to have good and bad days. Even small things may bother them. In the first two or three grades children may come home upset, without realizing what went wrong. Reassure them, and the story may come out eventually. In international schools most children are considerate of newcomers because they were also new at one time, but they can also be brutal at times, and newcomers are unsure and vulnerable, especially if changing schools has meant changing languages. If your children are harassed or bullied, speak to their teachers and school administrators.

Changing schools may be most difficult in the preadolescent period. Some studies have shown that children who have changed schools as early adolescents are less positive about school and themselves. In any case, children of this age will probably need extra support. Watch their relationships with teachers carefully, as these are important to children at this age.

Transitions

Discuss a move with your children. Take their input seriously. Let them make minor decisions. Keep them informed of plans. Friendships deepen with age, and it becomes more important for children to acknowledge these friendships and their sadness at leaving their friends. However, children often are not yet skilled in emotional work. Encourage them to express their feelings, and suggest ways to say goodbye. The older they are, the more children may have invested in their various activities. Research your new posting to see if it is possible for them to continue those activities.

Family is still at the center of children's lives. Parents can therefore help children adapt to a new country emotionally and physically and deal with their sadness and anger. Be sympathetic and encouraging. Children often need logistical support, a ride to friends' homes, or help in finding an activity they like.

To help schoolchildren:

- *Discuss a move.* Listen to your children's feelings about the move. Let them make minor decisions.
- *Be understanding.* Children have difficulty coping with different sets of rules. Encourage them to become proficient in applying the rules in appropriate situations.
- *Provide logistical support* to help children get involved in activities and make friends.
- *Encourage children to express emotions appropriately.*
- *Watch school transitions carefully.* If children seem to be having difficulty with teachers or other children, seek help from the school.

Adolescence (12–19 Years)

Adolescents have a lot to achieve in a relatively short time. They must move from childhood to adulthood, physiologically, cognitively and socially. They must gain the skills that enable them to become fulfilled and productive adults. Adolescence is often considered a time of rebellion and turmoil, but studies show that most adolescents report that relationships between them and their parents are quite positive. Adolescents continue to look to their parents for advice and guidance—at least at times. However, they can also be moody, although their moods don't usually last long. Their feelings are often intense, partly because many of the things that happen in adolescence evoke strong emotions—the first kiss, driving lessons, important exams. Adolescents moving to a new country face additional factors that can set off emotional reactions: leaving friends, starting at a new school, getting around a new country, being lonely, learning a new language. Outbursts, mood swings, and moodiness are normal reactions to these changes. However, if moods last for days or children are habitually depressed, talk to them and, if necessary, get professional help. Moving abroad overwhelms the coping abilities of some children.

Communicate with adolescents. Most will talk if we listen and avoid passing judgment or lecturing. Teenagers often don't share everything with us, and we must respect their need for privacy. They also like to choose their own times for talking—while you're cooking, for instance, or when they come in late at night. It's not always easy to be available at these times, but keeping lines of communication open is important. Adolescents need a good relationship with their parents, particularly abroad, where friends come and go. Open lines of communication can also help us judge when they need help.

Relationships

Adolescent friendships fulfil many functions. Friends swap ideas, talk about intimate subjects, and provide social support. Losing old friends therefore becomes more significant and finding new ones more difficult. Fortunately, teenagers are able to keep in touch with old friends through e-mail and telephones. Teenagers who have moved before, have often developed strategies for getting to know people—joining in sports or activity groups, taking the initiative in relating to others, persisting until they find suitable friends.

> Michelle says, "I told Svetlana how I felt about Jörg and then she went and told the other girls. I was really angry, but she didn't understand at all. She said, 'but they're your friends too. Why shouldn't I tell them?'"

Cultural differences can cause misunderstandings and misjudgments. Children may think that a person is suited to them but then find out that this is not the case. There are also cultural differences in ideas about how friends should behave toward each other, but expatriate adolescents often find that cultural differences are not the most important criteria in choosing friends. Older adolescents in particular seek friends with similar interests, ideas, and values, regardless of culture and country.

> Rolf says, "We never knew what stand the children were going to take on any topic. It depended a lot on what friends they had at the time or who they'd talked to last at school. At various times Oliver was pro-Palestinian, then pro-Israeli, pro-American and anti-American. He argued for and against the European Union, sanctions on Iraq, and NATO bombings of Serbia. It was really tiring at times because he was always adamant, no matter what side he was taking, but he probably learned a lot about the different issues and he certainly learned to see things from different perspectives."

The influence of peer pressure increases up until about the age of 15. Expatriate adolescents are often influenced by friends from other cultures. They try out their friends' ideas and allegiances and can go from one end of the political spectrum to the other. Encourage children to experiment with ideas and perspectives, even though discussions with teenagers can be tiring. Young teenagers in particular think in black and white. If they are right, you can't be. Only as they develop cognitively are they able to accept different arguments, perspectives, and shades of gray. And as they develop emotionally, they are better able to admit that you have a good point or even that they are wrong. In the long run, many children, even expatriates, often develop ideas that are not different from ours, but it is important for them to reach these positions on their own. The ability to accept other perspectives, even when you don't share them, is an important part of an international personality.

School

The older children are, the more difficult it becomes to change schools. There is less time to get used to new systems or catch up on things that they didn't cover at their last school. Learning a new language becomes far more difficult. The language level needed in high school is much more complex than that used in primary school, and students may fall behind in other subjects while they are learning the new language. Many international schools do not accept high school students who do not already speak the language of instruction. Social integration also becomes more difficult. As a result, many expatriate parents try to avoid moving during their children's high school years, at least the last two years.

Transitions

When moving, we cannot help adolescents the way we can help younger children. Every aspect of their lives has become more complex. School transitions are more difficult. They have usually invested more in activities and friendships at home, and it takes longer to make friends because they now look for specific qualities in close relationships. Adolescents also want and need to be independent and to solve many of their own problems.

The parent's role is now to provide backup: the information teenagers need to learn their way around a new country, or transport to activities or places where they can meet others. We can provide a sympathetic ear for problems and encouragement when the going is tough. Starting at a new school can lead to a dip in self-confidence, so avoid anything that would further lower teenagers' self-esteem—comments about not having found friends yet, for instance, or how messy their rooms are or how inappropriately they are dressed. Concentrate instead on their strong points.

Parents are also the last line of defense for teenagers. We set the limits and make the rules that allow them to become independent safely. Moves during adolescence are not easy, and we should also be on the lookout for problems that adolescents cannot deal with. Some children adopt constructive strategies when they have problems, seeking information and taking advice, or looking for compromises. Others run away from problems or deny that they exist: "No, everything's fine. I just get bad grades because the tests are stupid." Some children become pessimistic or fatalistic, or lapse into depression. If children do not gradually recover from a move, begin a dialogue. Offer help and support. If necessary, seek professional help.

Leaving friends can cause intense grief. Adolescent relationships are deep and complex. When teenagers leave their friends, they don't just lose people to hang out with; they lose confidants and people with whom they feel safe sharing ideas or whom they rely on for various kinds of support. Encourage children to maintain contact with old friends. If it is possible for them to visit friends during vacations, help organize it. Because teenagers expect more from relationships, it is also harder for them to find new friends. They are fussier or get hurt when new friends don't measure up. We can't make friends for our children, but we can provide company when they are lonely. If your children have not yet made friends, organize some interesting outings or trips with them. Encourage them to become involved in activities in which they might meet peers with similar interests. Parents can also help pick up the pieces when things go wrong, being ready with sympathy and understanding for the strong feelings involved.

To protect the interests of adolescents:

- *Be there!* Adolescents will confide in parents if they listen, honor confidences, and respect privacy. However, they must be able to choose their own times.
- *Provide information and backup.* Adolescents are eager to regain competence and independence. Provide information about the new environment and logistical support.
- *Set limits that enable teenagers to become independent safely.*
- *Take your children's friendships seriously.* Teenage relationships are complex and fulfill a variety of important roles. The pain involved in leaving friends and making new ones is very real.
- *Watch for problems such as depression or drug or alcohol abuse.*

Chapter 11
Language Learning

Fifteen-year-old Megan says, "There are all these stories, like spy novels, about how people speak a language perfectly after a year, and about kids that speak lots of languages. I wish it were that easy. I've tried so hard to learn French, but people here still look at me like, 'Stop crucifying our language.' "

Expatriates are often criticized for not learning the language of their host country. It's a fair criticism. Many of us don't try to learn host-country languages, or we try and then give up. Learning a language takes a lot of time and effort, and we may become reasonably fluent just in time to move on. The same goes for our children, but there is more at stake for them than the convenience of being able to communicate in a host country. Growing up in an environment where they can't speak the language affects the social development of young children and the independence of older ones. On the other hand, learning too many languages can mean that children grow up without a real mother tongue. They may not become thoroughly proficient or comfortable in any one language.

Language learning in children should not be taken lightly. Learning a new language is a key to understanding others, and children who learn a new language also gain cognitive and linguistic flexibility. But they can't absorb one language after another without negative effects. Expatriate children are often faced with the need to learn many different languages as they move from country to country. Many use different languages at home and at school, as well as the host-country language. It is therefore important to plan children's language "careers." When you first go abroad, decide on an educational language for your children and try to keep them in schools that use this language for instruction. When offered a posting, consider the host-country language. Do your children already speak it? Can they learn it easily? If children must learn a new language, decide how to provide the necessary support for them and how to avoid negative effects.

Language Options

Sergey says, "We speak Russian and Georgian at home and our children have to speak English at school. They also learned a bit of Arabic and French because we lived in Muscat and they went to kindergarten in Nice. We are living in Vienna now and I know they should learn some German, but it is just too much."

Almost every expatriate family has to make language choices. It must decide which languages the children should or must learn and when and how they should be introduced. It's often not a free choice. Some children, for instance, have to learn another language because there is no schooling available in their mother tongue. Some families may already use more than one language at home. As a result, we must often make the most of complex situations. The main thing is to take the issue seriously and make the best possible decisions.

Education is an important issue. Ideally, children learn to read and write in their home language before doing so in other languages. Getting used to classroom communication is easier in the mother tongue, but for many expatriate children this is not possible. They begin school abroad, where the language spoken is different from the one at home. Children are better able to make this change if they have had a high level of contact with spoken and written language at home and have attended preschools and learned the basics of classroom communication, and if the schoool has a good language program for children with different mother tongues.

When moving abroad, many children have to change their educational language because there is no schooling available in their mother tongue. This takes time, and the need to make several language changes during their education will be a handicap. If you are likely to make several moves, choose one type of international school for your children so that they do not change educational languages during their time abroad. English, American, French, or German international schools are the most common, although the latter are not found in every major city.

Decide what languages to use at home. Using your mother tongue has a number of advantages. Parents communicate best in their own language, and it is important for children to learn to communicate with people at home. If children are planning to study in their home country, it is essential for them to maintain proficiency in this language. However, bilingual families may be confronted with a situation in which children must understand too many languages — two languages at home, one at school, and various others in host countries. Some children do not cope well with this situation, and it may be better to choose one home language or have one person use the school language, if possible. If you decide to use two languages at home, stick to the rule of one person, one language.

Learning host-country languages often becomes a lower priority. For families that move often, learning all the host-country languages is rarely a viable option. Choose languages that are most useful in the long term—that are used in other countries as well, for instance, or that children can study as a school subject. Sometimes children make choices. They like a particular language or are motivated to learn it for some reason. Learning a host-country language has many advantages, especially if children are not already coping with several other languages. Or children can learn enough of a language to get by.

To choose languages wisely:

- *Make conscious language choices.* What will your children's educational language be? What languages should you speak at home? Set language priorities.
- *Try not to change your children's educational language,* at least while abroad.
- *Introduce languages appropriately.* If more than one language is used at home, each parent should speak only one language with the children.
- *Avoid **too** many languages.* Ensure that your children acquire a strong educational language, one in which they can read and write at a high level. They should have at least one language in which they can express themselves well.
- *Be sensitive to your children's abilities.* Not all children learn languages equally well. Observe your children carefully. Get help for them if they need it. Accept their limitations.

Learning a New Language

Learning another language is a long-term project even for children. Although young children often pick up languages easily and are soon happily conversing with the people around them, this is probably because they are less inhibited and need only a small vocabulary. However, studies repeatedly show that it takes children three to seven years to bring a second language up to the level of the first language or the level required for a good education.

Paula says, "My Mom spoke French at home and my Dad Swiss-German. I went to a local school in Spain and then to an international school, where I had to use English. I like being able to speak a lot of languages, but sometimes I feel that I can't really express myself in any of them."

Children need at least one language in which they are competent and comfortable. Humans are verbal creatures. We think, communicate, and even dream in words. Language helps us regulate our emotional life. "I am feeling depressed today" helps us sort out how we are feeling as well as communicate it to others. In giving our children linguistic keys to the world, we should be careful not to deprive them of the keys to their inner world. Children should also be able to speak, read, and write at least one language at a high level so that they can get a good education.

Not all children learn languages equally well. It's not always the brightest children who learn languages easily. Language learning requires a different set of skills from those needed to learn other subjects, and sometimes children who normally do well at school are upset when they find themselves not doing as well as usual. Children with some types of learning problems have difficulty learning another language. If your child has such problems, discuss them with an educational psychologist. Be sensitive to your children's abilities and provide encouragement and support if they are having trouble. Talk to teachers about how best to provide help.

Raising Bilingual or Multilingual Children

If you are excited about learning languages, your children are more likely to be excited as well. Children who grow up in a household in which speaking other languages is considered a good thing will be more enthusiastic about learning languages. If you try to communicate with people abroad, your children will make more of an effort too. They often take pleasure at learning faster than their parents and will correct you when you make a mistake. Allow them this small reward for their efforts. One sure way to motivate them to learn a language is to discuss things you *don't* want them to understand in that language!

Children need support from parents to learn other languages — either to learn the new language or to maintain their mother tongue. Multilingual children need a "language-rich" environment because what they hear in one language they do not hear in another. Children listening to someone speaking Swahili, for instance, learn new words in that language but not in English — although there are some crossovers; new concepts and grammatical constructions learned in one language promote their development in the second, for example. To acquire the same vocabulary and expertise in Swahili *and* English, they must hear more language. And to learn a language really well they need to hear all the forms: dialogue, songs, stories, and more. They must hear nuances of speech and how it is used in different situations. We don't talk to family members at home the way we talk to someone in a government office, for instance. To use language appropriately we need different vocabularies, tones of voice, and levels of formality for different situations. Expose children to as much language as possible. Hold conversations with them. If you have child care providers, encourage them to chat with your children and tell stories.

To learn a language, children need:

- *To hear all forms of language* — spoken language, stories, songs, poems, riddles, rhymes.
- *To experience verbal interaction in different contexts* — at home, in a restaurant, on the street, with friends, in official situations.
- *Conversational opportunities* with you, relatives, friends, household personnel, others.

Make learning a positive experience. Children learn better when they are rewarded for doing well rather than penalized for making mistakes. Children make mistakes even when they are learning only one language, and they make a lot more when they have more than one language to cope with. They mix languages or use a word from another language if they don't know it in the language they are using. If they are made to feel stupid every time they make a mistake, they may lose heart and stop trying. Provide models of language use rather than criticizing. If a child says, "We founded it," give the correct form without interrupting the conversation, "Yes, you found it in the garden, didn't you?" Children also need encouragement when others are negative—for example, when someone in a shop is rude because they took a long time to say what they wanted. Recognize their frustration, but congratulate them for trying. If they are willing, practice the correct form to use next time.

> We thought it would be great for the children to learn some Russian, so we sent them to a teacher twice a week, but it was horrible. They just repeated things over and over, and when they got something wrong the teacher whacked the table in front of them with a stick. Our 8-year-old was terrified.

Choose language teachers and schools carefully. Make sure the language learning takes place in a positive environment, even if teaching styles are different from what you are accustomed to. Children do not learn well when they are afraid of making mistakes. Punitive environments can damage self-confidence. Make sure your children are learning the skills that will be most useful to them: oral skills if they just need to get around in the host enviromnent; reading and writing if they need these skills when they return to their home country.

Encouraging Learning of Host-Country Languages

Speaking a host-country language is a big advantage for expatriate children. They experience a more normal social environment because they can communicate with all sorts of people, rather than just teachers and friends at school and parents at home. Teenagers can be more independent. They can ask directions when they get lost or order tickets for the movie theatre, for instance. They can participate in a wider range of activities and have a larger choice of friends.

At the same time, we have to be practical. Most of us are in a host country for only a limited time, and language learning is a long-term project. Consider how long you will be staying. Can the language be used in other countries? How much time do the children have available for language learning? Teenagers in their last year or two of school may not have a lot of free time. And how many languages do they already speak? Language learning also is more important in some countries than others. In some places it's hard to get around without knowing at least a little of the language. In others, people are more anxious to practice their English on you than to have you practice their language on them. Some languages are simply more difficult to learn than others.

Help your children acquire a survival vocabulary. It is not always possible or advisable for children to learn the host-country language, but even a few phrases can help them move around and provide some positive contacts. They should at least learn the courtesy phrases, such as "Hello" and "Goodbye," "Excuse me," and "Please" and "Thank-you." Older children need to be able to get around, to ask how to get somewhere or tell someone they are lost. It helps if they learn to read a few words, such as *exit* or *toilet.*

We can't expect our children to learn a host-country language if we don't. Start learning the host-country language yourself and make it a family affair. Practice greetings or short phrases on each other. Go on outings so the children can try out what they have learned. Avoid expressing negative attitudes toward the host country, and learn about the culture so that you can put language in context. Encourage your children to watch local TV.

Maintaining a Mother Tongue

For most people, using their mother tongue at home is best. Children who use the same language at home and at school have an advantage, but unless the parents have an excellent grasp of the school language, speaking their own language at home is usually still a better choice. We have the greatest depth of knowledge and feeling in that language. Few of us can communicate as well in another language. We don't have the same vocabulary or feeling for nuances, let alone a store of stories or children's songs and rhymes. As children's early linguistic skills are learned at home, they must have a good language model to imitate. Most expatriate children also go home at some time to study or work, and they need to be able to function at a high level in the home-country language. It is an important part of their identity as well as their cultural heritage. In bilingual families, consider how to expose children to both languages. The language of the parent who is away from home usually suffers, so if possible make it the language that the parents speak to each other so that the children hear it as much as possible.

At home, children learn a mother tongue from many different people. Abroad, they learn it mostly from us. Talk to your children about all sorts of things. Sing; read stories; quote writers, poets, and philosophers. Encourage your children to talk by taking time to listen well. What children hear in emotionally intense moments is often remembered best. Warm, exciting, or fun times improve learning—just as children remember the expletives we use when we are angry!

> Tatiana said she didn't want to go back to Moscow for the holidays, that she couldn't speak Russian any more. She said she didn't have the words for things. I asked her for an example and it was something she had only just learned in English, so of course she couldn't say it in Russian.

Children use increasingly sophisticated language as they grow older. They use more complex grammatical constructions and a larger vocabulary. If they are studying in another language, they sometimes feel that they have forgotten their mother tongue because they can't express themselves in it. In fact, their vocabulary simply grows faster in their educational language, and academic language relies more on explicit expression than does home language. To help your children "keep up" in their home language, discuss more complex issues with them in their mother tongue. Encourage them to read literature in that language and to watch videos and TV programs that use more sophisticated language, such as documentaries or the news.

> Carlos told me not to speak Spanish when he brought friends
> home from school, so I didn't, but I am not so good in English. When the friends go it is okay again. We speak Spanish. I am not angry but I am sad.

Children sometimes want to be just like everyone else and don't want to use another language in front of others. This can be a function of the environment. Some countries are more accepting of bilingualism than others, as are schools. Sometimes it is just a function of being part of a social group, so don't get upset if your children don't want to use your language in some situations. They will probably also want to be different sometimes and use "their" language. Be sensitive to their preferences, but encourage them to speak your language in other situations. Make it fun: Play language games; get videos or computer games. Children's use of each language often depends on the situation. They gossip in the school language and discuss family matters in the home language, for instance.

To encourage foreign-language learning:

- *Value language learning.* Be positive about learning other languages. Make language learning a family affair.
- *Create a language rich environment.* Converse with your children. Encourage them to interact with others. Provide more sophisticated linguistic opportunities as the children grow older.
- *Ensure that your children acquire a strong educational language* in which they can read and write at a high level.
- *Ensure that your children have at least one language in which they can express themselves.* Humans are verbal creatures. We need to be able to identify and communicate our emotions.
- *Be flexible.* Accept your children's language preferences.
- *Choose teachers and schools carefully.* Children learn best in a positive environment.

Chapter 12
Schools

Roberta says, "Our four children attended five international schools altogether, and they were all quite different. The one we all liked best was quite small, with only 300 children from K–12, but it was a happy school. The principal really wanted all the kids and teachers to get along with each other. He believed that international education was something special. Unfortunately, after three years he moved to another school because of a conflict with the school board."

*S*chooling is an important issue for parents moving abroad. Many parents hesitate to accept an overseas assignment because they not want to risk their children's education, but in general, being educated abroad is good for children, at least academically. A study of hundreds of American college-age students who had been expatriate children found they that were four times more likely to earn a bachelor's degree than the national average.* However, there are special challenges associated with education abroad, and schools should be chosen with care.

Most expatriate parents send their children to international schools. These schools cater primarily to expatriate children and can be found in most large cities around the world. However, local schools have advantages in some cases. Some parents prefer boarding schools or home schooling, or leave their children in the care of friends or relatives. Unfortunately, there are few options for children with significant special needs.

As soon as a transfer becomes a possibility, find out what schools are available. Contact potential schools immediately, as many international and private local schools have waiting lists. Some give preference to specified groups of people, such as diplomats, depending on their mandate.

Plan children's educational careers abroad carefully. You may not be able to predict what your next posting will be, but most organizations have transfer patterns. How long is the average transfer period, for instance? Is this a one-time transfer, or will you eventually move to other countries as well? If you are only staying in a country a year or two, choose the schooling option that requires the fewest adjustments. Most children can change school systems and learn new languages, but this takes more time. If you are likely to make several moves abroad, your children should stay in the same school system—American, British, or French—through all your moves, or at least in schools that use the same language. If you are planning to stay in one country a long time, or if your children have already been attending school in the host-country language, local schools have certain advantages.

---

* This study was undertaken by Dr. Anne Baker Cottrell, Drs. John Useem and Ruth Hill Useem, and Kathleen Finn Jordan. According to this study of 680 adult third culture kids, 81 percent earned a bachelor's degree and half of this number went on to earn master's degrees or doctorates.

International Schools

International schools cater primarily to expatriate children. They typically have students from 30 to 50 countries, but sometimes
more than 100 countries are represented. In most schools the
majority of students come from all over the world rather than
from any one country. In many American or British schools,
25–30 percent of the students are from the home country and
10–20 percent from the host country; the latter are children of
wealthy local people, mixed marriages, or former expatriates.
Almost all international schools are independent and each is
different, but there are several basic types.

Types of international schools:

- *"National" international schools* have a system based on
  a home-country system, most commonly the United
  States, Britain, or France, and the majority of teachers
  are from that country. Students of other nationalities
  are accepted depending on their language skills.
- *"International" international schools* strive for a
  multicultural environment. Many use International
  Baccalaureate curriculum guides at all levels. The
  teachers come from many countries.
- *Organization schools* cater to the employees of an
  organization; examples include U. S. military, United
  Nations, and NATO schools. Companies with large
  projects sometimes sponsor schools. Many are open to
  outsiders if space is available.

*International schools represent a variety of nationalities and edu-
cational philosophies.* The most common international schools
with national affiliations are American, British, and French,
with a smaller number of German schools. Other nationalities have a few schools scattered around the world.* Most
schools are independent and have been established under a

---

* These include Swiss, Italian, Indian, Japanese, Korean, Dutch, and
  Turkish schools.

variety of conditions, such as private, parent-owned, or non-profit. Some national schools receive limited government financing from a home country or are company-sponsored. These conditions affect the mandate of the school — whom it was established to serve and the school's philosophy.

Many international schools prepare students for graduation under more than one system — for the American diploma as well as the British GSCE examinations, for instance. Increasing numbers of schools offer the curriculum and preparation for the International Baccalaureate (IB) examination, which is accepted by many countries as a qualification for university acceptance. "National" international schools are usually accredited by educational authorities in the home country, which are often regional rather than national. This means that a German school in Buenos Aires, for example, may not be quite the same as one in Paris because the schools are accredited by different regional bodies. French schools, however, adhere to a national curriculum wherever they are located.

> Pontus says, "I didn't even feel I had a cultural identity until I came here [to an international school]. I never talked about my country in the local school here. No one wanted to know, and I just tried to be like everyone else. Here, where you're from is a daily topic. I like feeling that I'm from somewhere."

All international schools provide some opportunities to explore cultural identity, an important issue for expatriate children. However, "national" international schools reflect the educational philosophies of their parent countries and were originally established to provide an American or British or French education abroad. Students attending these schools will assimilate many of the educational and cultural mores of these countries. "International" international schools also have a "school culture," but they aim for a more multicultural atmosphere.

International schools cater to mobile children, generally accepting students at any time of the year if there is room. With annual turnovers of up to 30 percent, they have experience in helping students adjust. Most organize orientation events for new students at the beginning of the year. Other students know what it feels like to be new, and because of the high turnover, social groups tend to be less rigid. Most of these schools run programs for students who speak languages other than the one used in school.

International schools have some disadvantages. They are often isolated from the host community, limiting the opportunities for children to learn the local language and culture. High student turnover means that children regularly have to say goodbye to friends and classmates. These schools are also designed for college- or university-bound students, with few vocational courses. Most do not cater to students with special needs. They are also expensive. As independent, private, or parent-owned nonprofit organizations that hire a majority of teachers from abroad, their overheads are high. Some national international schools receive support from home countries, but this usually amounts to a small part of the budget. Most parents rely on help from their employers to pay school fees.

The International Baccalaureate

The International Baccalaureate Organization (IBO) offers a standardized examination that is accepted as an entry requirement for universities in many countries. Students are encouraged to also study their mother tongue by means of outside tutors or correspondence, if necessary, so that they can attend universities or find work in their own country. Many U.S. universities accept IB certificates as the equivalent of Advanced Placement (AP) programs.

The IB program leading to the examination covers the last two years of high school, but many schools have also adopted the curriculum for primary and middle school (IBPYP and IBPMP). This program encourages an international perspective as well as community responsibility. Unfortunately, it does not cater to vocational students and does not include a sports program for less academically oriented students.

Local Schools

Local schools provide an opportunity to learn the language and culture of the host country, but language learning and integration take time. If the host-country language is different from the home-country language, local schools are not an option for expatriates who will spend three years or less in that country. An exception is young children, who adapt more rapidly and don't face the same academic challenges as older children.

Types of local schools:

- *Host-country public schools,* in which the language of instruction is the host-country language. The European Union also promotes the establishment of European schools with instruction in various member-country languages.
- *Host-country private schools* are usually cheaper than international schools and often are in a better position than public schools to help new students integrate. They are also an option in countries with inadequate public school systems.

Young children adapt more easily. Attending a local kindergarten or the first year or so of school is much easier than changing school systems and languages at a higher level. Although young children do not learn languages faster than adolescents, they have a lot less to learn—a much smaller vocabulary and less complex grammar. And they have plenty of time to catch up if they fall behind in other subjects while they are learning the school language. Getting to know other children is also easier, and young children accept new social mores more readily.

> A Russian couple, Igor and Irina, put their three children in a local bilingual (Greek/English) school in Cyprus. The children had previously attended other English-language schools, and the parents welcomed the opportunity for their

children to learn a third language. A year later they were frantically searching for alternatives. All three children had struggled unsuccessfully with Greek, did not get along with the other children, and were profoundly unhappy.

In any country it takes a while for foreigners to be accepted. Whether foreign students are met with interest or with hostility depends to some extent on the school, as well as on the degree of racism or xenophobia prevailing in a country. It also depends on the individuals children come into contact with. Sometimes they are lucky and are accepted into a group of other children immediately, or find a tolerant and understanding teacher. Talk to other foreigners with children in the school you are considering. Do faculty members seem happy to have your children in the school? What feeling do you get when you visit?

The educational philosophy will reflect the local culture, from how students are expected to behave and learn to the involvement of parents in the school. Make sure that you can come to terms with the main parameters of the educational system. Children will also adopt attitudes and ideas from the local community, confronting us with new ways of doing things. Foreign children may submerge their own national identities in order to fit in.

Local schools are less accustomed to helping new students fit in. The students have often been together for years, and the social groups are less open. On the other hand, friends are less likely to move away, and when you finally leave the country, your children will always have friends to write to or visit. Private local schools can be a good compromise. They are usually less expensive than international schools but are often smaller and have the smaller classes and more individual attention that help children adjust.

Other Options

Some countries have no suitable schools, and parents must either refuse the posting or look for other options. These include boarding schools, home schooling, and leaving children at home or at the previous posting. Some parents make these choices so that their children do not to have to learn a new educational language.

Boarding Schools

Sending children away to school is a choice for some, a necessity for others. Boarding schools are an integral part of Britain's school tradition, for example, but an unfortunate necessity for other parents—because there are no schools at a new posting, because the political situation is unstable, or because the parents expect to be transferred often. Boarding schools at home are not the only option. Many parents prefer to have their children attend a boarding school that is closer to them, in their host country or a third country.

> Spiros and Anna were surprised that Chris chose a strict, traditional boarding school. Spiros says, "He's always been to American schools and we thought he would choose a relaxed school, but he chose one where they have uniforms and at four o'clock you do this and at five o'clock that. Anyway, he hasn't complained so far, except about the food."

Children adjust better if they have some say in decisions that will affect them. Make a list of the schools that you are considering, visit them if possible, and get your children's input. Older children should make their own choices. If children are really opposed to going to boarding school, consider alternatives. Don't accept the posting, consider home schooling, or delay the move to boarding school for a year or two.

Even children who are enthusiastic about going to boarding school may have mixed feelings when the moment comes. Help them say goodbye to their old life and prepare for the new one. Be positive. Tell them how much you will miss them but how glad you are that they have the opportunity to get a good education and participate in many activities.

Settling in takes time. If children are distressed, listen carefully but keep in mind that you may be talking to them at their worst moments. Homesickness tends to be worst at night, for instance, and children may be relatively happy during the day. Stay in close contact with the school. School personnel have experience dealing with new children and should be able to judge whether your children are having more difficulty than others—but you should have the last word.

Children change quickly, and absent parents must keep up. Keeping in touch has become easier, thanks to modern technology. Communicate with your children often and in as many ways as you can—phone calls, e-mails, letters, packages, visits. Try to catch some of their special moments. Attend important events if possible, or ask your children to send videos, take photos, or write about their activities. When the children come home, take time to listen to them and catch up on their ideas and interests.

Home Schooling, Correspondence, Cyberschool

Expatriates choose home schooling for a variety of reasons: They live in remote locations; the available schools are inadequate; they don't want their children to change educational languages or systems: they are abroad for only a short time; or their children have special needs. Check the host country's laws about home schooling so that you do not run afoul of the local educational authorities.

Home schooling requires time and commitment. Abroad, it takes more planning. Materials usually have to come from the home country, and it is more difficult to organize outings and social events because of language differences. Some countries provide correspondence courses for nationals who are living in remote locations or spending a limited time abroad. Private organizations offer everything from support packages and materials to online tutoring. Several specialize in schooling for expatiate children.

Staying Home, Staying Behind

Sixteen-year-old Steven says, "I really wanted to stay behind in Germany. Friends said I could stay with them,

but my Dad just didn't want it. He said I still needed the
family and they needed me. My little sister was sure upset
at the idea of my staying behind. We had a lot of arguments
about it and eventually I just gave in. Maybe Dad was right.
It's good that he was willing to discuss—well, actually ar-
gue—it out with me."

*Leaving children behind is a sensible option to consider in the last
year or two of school.* Many 16- to 18-year-old students have
difficulty adjusting, both academically and socially. If possible,
parents and organizations should avoid moves during the last
two years of school. If it can't be avoided, consider leaving
children with friends or relatives, especially if they are not
doing well at school or have difficulty adjusting.

Choosing a School

Maira, Claude, and 10-year-old David studied the information about schools in Singapore. They found a school
that they all liked and decided to enroll David during their
apartment-hunting trip, but their school visit was disap-
pointing. The facilities were impressive, but the atmosphere
was stiff and the classrooms were bare. They were also put
off by the principal's arrogant and condescending tone. They
hastily made an appointment with the second school on
their list.

*When you have decided on the type of school you prefer, look at the
individual schools if there is a choice.* Get as much information
as possible. If your organization allows "look-see" visits, make
visiting schools a high priority even if your children are not
with you. Don't be afraid to ask questions. If you are not really fluent in the school language, take along an interpreter.
Talk to other parents or students if possible.

Sources of information about schools:

- *The Internet.* Many international schools have web sites.
  The European Council of International Schools (ECIS)
  lists hundreds of international schools at www.ecis.org.

Many public schools are also listed on the Internet, but it is not possible to list all of their sites here.

- *A directory* of overseas schools, covering around 800 schools, is published by International Schools Services (ISS).
- *International schools* near you should have a copy of the ISS directory. Ask about teachers or parents who have first-hand experience of the schools in your new country.
- *Many embassies* have lists of the schools that their young nationals attend.
- *Relocation companies* with expatriate services have information about schools and can help you identify the best school for your children. Unfortunately, these services must be paid for.

The following features contribute to a good school. Get information about as many of these points as possible. Information about the "hardware" of a school—location, facilities, class size, activities offered—is relatively easy to find. The "software"—educational philosophy, academic standards, faculty, social environment—is more readily available if you can visit the school or talk to other expatriates.

Features of Schools

Hardware:

- *Location.* Is the school in a safe area? Is it located in an expensive rental area? How long does it take to get to the school? How can children get to school? School buses often have long routes. How long would your children spend on a bus? How can they get to activities and social events at the school?
- *Building.* Is the school itself a healthy environment with enough space, light, and ventilation? Is heating adequate? In hot countries, is air conditioning available?
- *Facilities.* Check the library, computer, and sports facilities. These facilities may be the only ones available to your child. The library may be the only one in the city with books in English, for instance.

- *Size.* The number of students in international schools ranges from a few students to 1,500, with an average of 300–600. Small schools are more personal, and children are able to integrate faster. Larger schools offer a better selection of courses, social groups, facilities, and activities, but children often take longer to integrate and may find it harder to get onto school teams and the like.
- *Class size.* Teachers can give students more personal attention in small classes. In international schools, where teachers must cope with many new students as well as students who speak other languages, the student/teacher ratio should be less than 20/1 and preferable between 12/1 and 15/1.
- *Teaching materials.* Schools should be well stocked with teaching and learning materials. Textbooks should not be more than five years old, particularly in the case of science texts.

Software:

- *Educational philosophy/cultural environment.* Many schools have an explicit educational philosophy, but this is also influenced by the nationalities of administrators, teachers, and students. Ask what nationalities are represented. These are the cultural influences your children will be exposed to.
- *Curriculum.* Ask for an outline of what is covered in each subject in your children's grades. This will help you see how they will fit in academically. A flexible and individualized curriculum serves students from different backgrounds.
- *Activities.* Because of language differences, your child may not be able to participate in activities in the local community. It is therefore important that an international school offer a range of after-school activities.
- *Community.* Expatriate children's lives rotate around school. Good international schools function as communities, welcoming teachers, students, and parents. As a parent, do you feel welcome in the school? Are your concerns taken seriously? Schools should also be

proactive in dealing with the conflicts that arise when students of many nationalities are brought together.

- *Specialists.* Schools that cater to expatriate children need specialist teachers for languages and for children with special needs, as well as counselors.

Annette says, "Pierre has always gone to French schools, but André didn't do well in these schools so we sent him to American schools. They both did well, but when we went back to Canada, it just wasn't possible to keep Pierre in a French school. It was just too far away."

What others consider the best school may not be best for your child. Children have different educational backgrounds, temperaments, and needs. Some children need a lot of structure. Others need a creative atmosphere. Finding schools for several children in a family is challenging. International schools are often K–12, so all children can attend the same school. Siblings then have each other for support, and it simplifies transportation and attendance at school activities. However, there is not always space for all children at a school, and some children have different needs that may be better met at another school.

To choose a school:

- *Consider the school facilities.* These are more important abroad because they may be the only ones available to your children.
- *Consider school culture and atmosphere.* School culture influences children's social and cultural development. Abroad, school is the center of children's social life, so the school atmosphere is doubly important.
- *Choose the best school for your children.* Listen to other people's advice, but make your own decisions. You know your children best.

Settling In

Seventeen-year-old Kyle says, "I hope there are some new students this year. We've all been here since ninth grade and it's getting boring. We need some new blood."

Students at international schools are used to welcoming new students. Almost all of them were new at some time, and because they haven't been together very long, social groups are looser. Most schools have a system for integrating new students — an orientation for new students before the school year starts, for instance. Some schools have a buddy system in which each new student is teamed up with another student. Teachers help students assimilate.

Local schools are less often in a position to help foreign students assimilate. Local schools, teachers, and students are not used to helping new students settle down, but there are always individuals who will go out of their way to help new children. After we fled Liberia, our daughter attended school in a Swiss village. Her teacher encouraged the other students to help her in class and include her in the playground. In the beginning she was allowed to write her essays in English.

Children cannot do everything at once. Settling down in class, catching up on material they may not have covered in their last school, and getting used to a new home and country is a lot to cope with. Encourage your children to join in activities, but be understanding if they just try one and say they'll start something else next semester.

Ease of assimilation in international schools can depend on nationality. Nationality-based cliques do exist, especially among young adolescents or where there are a large number of students of one nationality. Children who are the only ones of their nationality in the school may find it more difficult to assimilate. There is also a certain consciousness of parents' occupations — whether they are part of the diplomatic, business, or missionary communities, for instance. Parents can help break down such barriers. Encourage your children to interact with all sorts of others. Welcome other children into your home. Get to know other parents. This is to the children's advantage. International schools are often small, and children who spend time only with others of the same nationality have a limited number of potential friends.

Get involved in the school. International schools welcome involvement. In local schools you will have to find the best way to get involved. Many schools, both international and local, have parents' associations. Volunteers may be welcome to help in classrooms or accompany children on field trips. This is a good way to get to know teachers and other parents and see how the school works. If you have the appropriate training, there may be jobs available at the school. Substitute teachers are always welcome, for instance. Knowing that you are nearby is comforting for many children, although teenagers might prefer not to have you around all the time.

To help children settle in at school:

- *Don't expect your children to do everything at once,* especially if they have to learn a new language. They may not join in new activities immediately or keep up old ones.
- *Encourage your children to mix with children of other nationalities.* Children profit from cross-cultural contact and have a larger social group if they can accept and get along with children from other cultures.
- *Get involved in the school.* This will help you get to know the school, teachers, and other parents. Most children feel more comfortable if their parents are involved in the school.

Changing Educational Languages

The decision to change educational languages should not be taken lightly. Children who must learn another language in order to attend a new school are being asked to make a major adjustment. They must learn not only the language but also the school culture: how information is learned, analyzed, and presented, and how to relate to teachers and other students. This gets harder with age. The language used in higher grades is more complex. A kindergarten child can get by on a 100-word vocabulary, not so a tenth-grader. Older students also miss more material in other subjects while they are learning the new language, and they have less time to catch up before graduation.

*Most international schools offer special programs for chil-
dren who speak other languages.* Students who arrive at a
school speaking no English usually spend all day in the language department for several months. As soon as they have
a grasp of the language, they receive instruction in other
subjects, either in the language department or in normal
classes. It is important for students not to fall too far behind in other subjects while they are learning a new language. They usually begin with math and science classes,
in which fewer language skills are needed.

*Students have to learn not only a new language but new ways of
doing things.* Education includes many cultural features. In
some systems, for instance, students must learn information
and then reproduce it as accurately as possible. In others,
students are encouraged to learn information but to present
it in their own words. Reproducing the work of others may
be considered plagiarism. In American English, the writer is
expected to make his or her ideas clear. In other languages,
understanding is the primary responsibility of the reader. The
required structure and presentation of information is different from one school to another.

*Avoid requiring children to start school and learn a new language
at the same time.* Starting school, even preschool, is tough
enough for most children without being confronted with a
new language as well. If you can't avoid this situation, make
sure the children have a basic vocabulary before they start.
They should at least be able to ask to go to the toilet, for
instance. Children should already have had experience mix-
ing with others.

Language Courses

*Warm and welcoming language departments will provide a "safe"
area for new students.* In such an atmosphere students learn
better and get to know each other well. Language departments should offer a wide range of teaching tools: language
books, dictionaries, literature, magazines, and games.

A good language program provides:

- *A positive learning environment.* Children learn better when they feel comfortable and confident.
- *High expectations.* Some children learn languages more easily than others, but teachers should encourage *all* students.
- *Individualized programs.* Teachers should be able to individualize programs to accommodate students with different backgrounds and needs.
- *Programs should employ a variety of methods and materials* to develop all aspects of language and cater to different learning styles.
- *A student-centered approach.* Children's previous knowledge and abilities should be acknowledged and employed.

Parental Support

Children who are learning a new educational language need their parents' support. In the first few weeks they may come home upset or frustrated and need comfort and encouragement. Be understanding if they feel overwhelmed and do not manage other aspects of their lives well, like keeping their bedroom neat or practicing an instrument. If you don't speak the school's language well, you can still help your children. Studies show that parental support and encouragement is vital even when another language is spoken at home.

> Magdalena would come home from school and sleep for two hours. Then she would do homework and watch a video or something. She didn't want to talk about school or do anything else. I thought we had made a terrible mistake putting her in an English school, but after six weeks she started ballet classes and brought home a little Korean friend from her ESL class.

Spending all day among people who speak another language is frustrating. Several hours of language instruction a day are exhausting. Children who are learning a new language need encouragement and support from parents. After such a demanding day, they should not have to do several hours of homework. If they are spending too much time on homework or seem overwhelmed, talk to their teachers.

Mother Tongue

Sometimes children can study their mother tongue at school, but often they cannot. Some parents organize after-school lessons or tutoring for their children. However, if your children are changing their educational language, wait before starting such lessons. This is already a very strenuous time for them.

The International Baccalaureate program promotes mother tongue learning. Students are encouraged to take their mother tongue as a subject, either as a first language or as a foreign language, even if it means obtaining a tutor from outside the school. Check whether schools offer this program.

To support children learning another educational language:
* *Avoid changes in the last year or two of school.*
* *Avoid simultaneous school beginning and language change.* If this can't be avoided, make sure your child has a basic vocabulary. Spend some time in the classroom with your child.
* *Choose a school with a good language program.*
* *Provide support at home.* Show understanding when your children are tired or frustrated. Be positive toward teachers and the school. If your children are overwhelmed, talk to their teachers.

Children with Special Needs

Anna was a bright, lively 5-year-old, used to trying to keep up with her three older brothers. She also had Down syndrome. When her parents tried to register her at the international school attended by her brothers, the school refused to accept her. Although her parents were willing

to help in the classroom or to take Anna out of school if
there were problems or activities she could not participate in, the school remained firm.

*International schools do not cater to children with significant spe-
cial needs.* Many of these schools are small, and most are privately funded. Almost none have the facilities and staff to
cater to children with significant physical, psychological, or
mental difficulties. A few can provide help for children with
mild to moderate learning problems, and schools will generally accept students with physical disabilities if their facilities are suitable—for example, if they have an elevator that
can be used by a child in a wheelchair. A few European Union
schools have facilities for students with disabilities, and in
countries in which language is not a problem, children may
be able to attend local schools. Home schooling or correspondence schooling may be an option.

> Afraid his son would not be accepted when he enrolled the
> 6-year-old in an international school, Manuel's father did
> not mention that the boy had been receiving treatment for
> psychological problems. Six months later the parents were
> asked to take Manuel out of school. Despite help from the
> school counselor, his teacher could not control him. He dis-
> rupted the class daily, throwing chairs and books and lock-
> ing the teacher out of the classroom. Manuel's mother
> returned home with her son.

Be honest with schools about your children's needs so that they
can determine whether they can provide a suitable program
for them. If they can't, it is better to find out as soon as possible
rather than several months down the line. It is a terrible experience for children to struggle in a school and eventually be
rejected. It also puts the family in the difficult position of finding alternative schooling or returning home.

Learning Problems

*A few international schools have facilities for children with mild
learning problems* but can't deal with children with severe

problems. International schools are independent, with few outside resources, and can't finance the range of specialists needed to help children with severe problems. Language differences often make local specialists inaccessible. Before going abroad, have children with learning problems tested by an educational psychologist to find out what kinds of support they need. Schools need the psychologist's report as well as previous school reports to assess whether they can meet the needs of students with learning problems.

Some problems don't become obvious until children start school or begin to learn a second language. If your child develops problems and the school can't help, look for people with suitable training and experience within the expatriate or the local community. At the very least, you should be able to find tutors to help the child in specific subjects. Find out all you can about the condition—from the Internet, for instance. Start a support group in the school or in the community.

To help children with special needs:

- *Find out what your options are.* Consult specialists at home to identify your child's needs. Contact schools to see if they can meet your child's needs.
- *Locate extra support personnel* such as special education teachers or tutors.
- *Find out as much as you can about the disability.* There are many resources on the Internet.
- *Start a support group.* There may be children with similar disabilities. Contact their parents and arrange to swap ideas and information and provide mutual encouragement.

Chapter 13
Values

Brian upset his grandmother whenever they played games together. "He cheats," she said, "and he's not even ashamed when I catch him." Back in Africa, Brian's mother paid closer attention to the games he played with his nanny and realized that the giggling and laughter she heard occurred mostly when they managed to "out-cheat" each other. The real game was a test of wits that had little to do with the board or counters in front of them.

*W*hen we go abroad as adults, our cultural systems are well developed. They include sets of values we have learned from our family, friends, community, and country. Children growing up abroad will also be influenced by their environment, but this includes other-culture friends, schools, communities, and countries. While we consider new ideas in the light of an already established belief system, children have fewer of these beliefs through which to filter new impressions. As a result, they absorb different ways of thinking and behaving, and because they are still developing, these become part of their belief system and perspective on the world.

Expatriate children grow up able to understand other cultures in a way that we cannot. They are better able to walk in other people's shoes and take on different perspectives. These are keys to thriving abroad, and we must help them develop these skills, but how far should we take this? Should our children accept everything their friends believe or always approve of the way they behave? What values do we really want our children to have? What values *must* they have to guide their lives?

To live wisely and safely, children need ethical guidelines and a sense of moral purpose. Expatriate parents face the challenge of helping children grow up tolerant, but with their own set of beliefs and values to guide them. Fortunately, often these are not contradictory goals but a matter of common sense and balance.

Our Values

We often don't recognize our own values. Some parts of our belief system lie so deep that we don't consider them values but "just the way things are." We are not consciously aware of some underlying assumptions, such as those about God or about whether human beings are basically good or evil. But human civilizations are so diverse that there is almost nothing that some other culture does not think differently about. And we interpret the world according to these beliefs and values. They define the way we see the world, how we interpret events or judge people. People from different cultures often interpret the same situation differently. After a visit to a bazaar, for instance, we find that we have paid more than the going price for an item and therefore consider the vendor dishonest. He, on the other hand, may regard bargaining as an important skill and consider us a bit dimwitted.

Judy was shocked when 10-year-old Melanie got a zero on an assignment because she was caught cheating. Melanie protested, "Ayşe was really hurt when I wouldn't tell her the answers. She said she thought we were friends. You always said we should help people."

Values and beliefs often reveal themselves when someone does something differently than we do. We realize how important punctuality is to us when we live in a country where people are often late or don't arrive at all. We notice how we feel about family in a country in which work always comes first, or alternatively, where employees often miss work because they have to attend to family matters. And it really gets our attention when our children don't observe our values. We wonder where we went wrong or worry that they will not grow up "right." But we must understand that they are growing up in a different environment. We cannot expect them to do everything the way we do. It is not fair to get angry with them when they adapt to the environment we have put them in. On the other hand, we must provide them with some guidance.

Fortunately, when children do something different, it often is not serious. They acquire different manners, such as adopting table maners we are not comfortable with or using different social etiquette; greeting people in a more or less casual way then we do; using more or less *pleases* and *thank yous* than we think is appropriate; answering the phone in a way we do not really approve of. They try out different ideas, adopt political stances that are different from ours, or point out other perspectives on issues. These differences can expand our horizons. They make us think about the way we do things and force us to become aware of our expectations. However, there are also serious issues at stake. Children come into contact with different concepts of honesty, trust, or loyalty, for instance. They don't consider punctuality or a work ethic important. They question the tenets of our faith.

Anita started an environmental club at her son's school. "I wanted him to learn to respect the environment because here they are just ruining the beautiful places. They build

anything, anywhere and throw garbage all over the
place. The trucks belch out black smoke."

There are some beliefs and values that we feel we must pass on.
They are so central to our lives that we consider them critical for our children as well. We often assume that our children will automatically absorb these values as we did, but in
other countries they often observe a different set of cultural
mores in action. They are confused when we get upset because they have done something "wrong." We can avoid un-
necessary conflict if we identify our important values and
communicate them to our children.

Many beliefs are established early in life. As a result, family values are the first and most important influence on children, but
actions speak louder than words. We must live by our convictions if we want our children to adopt them. Young children
learn through observation, mimicking what they see around
them. They learn things—including values—by example. Even
older children are more likely to internalize and adopt the values that we live by rather than the ones we pay lip service to. If
we tell our children that they should be honest or trustworthy
or respect other people's privacy, but we don't do it ourselves,
they are less likely to take these values seriously.

> Anita says, "All Daros's other classmates had left for the
> summer. He kept nagging me to call David's mother to see
> if he could come and play. When I did and his mother said
> that David had enough children from his own country to
> play with, I was speechless. I didn't know what I should
> tell my son, either. David was such a nice boy, but he was
> not even allowed to go to his classmates' birthday parties."

*Some parents "solve" the problem by avoiding cross-cultural con-
tact.* They try to remove the influence of competing cultural
systems, but expatriate children inevitably come into contact
with culturally different individuals, in the host country or at
school. In most international schools, 60 percent or more of
the students come from different countries. To thrive in such
a multicultural environment, children need cross-cultural

skills, and parents who avoid such contacts deprive their children of the opportunity to learn these skills.

To transmit home values to children:

- *Think about your most important beliefs and values carefully.* If your children do something that upsets you, consider why. Have they contravened an important value?
- *Be patient.* Explain your beliefs and values to your children and explain why they are important to you. Discuss other people's beliefs and values openly.
- *Consider compromises.* Accept differences in peripheral values like manners, clothing, music, and so forth. Help your children learn home-country values, but don't get upset if they don't always adhere to these when you're abroad.
- *Live up to your beliefs and values.* Abroad we may be the only models of important values. The more we live up to them, the more our children will take them seriously.

Their Values

Living among people from other cultures has more impact on children than on adults. Expatriate children may form close relationships with host-country nationals, spending a lot of time in the company of household personnel or neighbors, for instance. At school they make friends from other cultures and adapt to the school culture. The values and beliefs of all these people influence children.

> Frederick's mother says, "We have been back at home for four years now, but Frederick still has a bazaar mentality. When I say "No," he thinks that's my opening bid. I tell him from the beginning whether something is open to negotiation or not—but there are also times when I wish I could negotiate the way he can."

Children have to get along with peers who are culturally different. The phrase "third culture kids" (TCKs) is often used for expatriate children. There are various explanations for this term, but in general it assumes that expatriate children meet each other on a kind of neutral ground. Sounds good, but where is this neutral ground? Is it a place where "anything goes"? Do children find that the only way to agree is to abandon their moral values so that they are all the same?

> Liz says, "During the NATO bombing of Serbia, Charles was all for it. That was what he heard at school and on TV. Then he had a music teacher he really liked who had been in Belgrade during the bombing and naturally had a different view. Charles thought about for it for a while and then one day he said, 'Nothing's really simple, is it?'"

Fortunately, expatriate children don't usually abandon all their values. They find many ways to reach agreement or live with disagreement. They don't expect their friends to be the same as they are. However, they are more likely to question everything, including home values. They try out other ideas and perspectives in searching for their own path. They may also modify their values in order to fit in with friends.

> Zahir says, "When I'm in Pakistan, I love being able to go and really bargain for things. I know that what I'm buying sometimes isn't what the guy says it is, but it's my own lookout if it's not. When I come back to Germany, though, I get really annoyed when something is not what it says on the label. It seems a lot more dishonest than in Pakistan somehow, because people expect it."

This is not an easy process. Weighing the pros and cons in connection with beliefs and values is complex. Many of us never had to do this. Growing up among people from a similar culture, we had no reason to question, or even recognize, much of what we believe. Our children do. And because their lives are different, they cannot just imitate us. At the same time, they still must develop a code to live by. They must reconcile different sets of beliefs and values. In many cases it is a question of where they stand on a continuum—how important privacy is, for instance, or how much responsibility they accept for their actions. Fortunately, relatively few values are mutually exclusive, and children also use their knowledge of other cultures to choose what is appropriate in each situation. Even so, they must make complex decisions and be able to live with answers that are not straightforward.

Parents can help. Children need to understand the meaning of values and their role in helping us live our lives. They need to discuss ideas and perspectives. If we listen to our children, we get to know what they think and have a chance to put forward our own views. We may also learn something. If we don't listen or refuse to accept their ideas, we lose these opportunities. In the long run, we cannot change the way our children choose to live, but we can set a good example and keep up the dialogue.

To help children develop their own values:

- *Discuss belief systems.* Take your children's ideas seriously. Talk about your own values and beliefs and why you hold them.
- *Expose your children to the ideas of philosophers, poets, and leaders that have inspired you.* Hang up inspirational, witty, or funny sayings—or send your children a text message on their mobile phones if that's the way to get their attention!
- *Be patient with experiments and mistakes.* Accept some deviations from your way of doing things. Discuss the pros and cons of various attitudes. Children learn better if they arrive at a conclusion on their own rather than being forced into it. If they make a mistake, discuss what went wrong.

Tolerance

…the human capacity to injure other people is very great precisely because our capacity to imagine other people is very small. —— *Elaine Scarry*[*]

---

[*] Scarry, Elaine. "The Difficulty of Imagining Other Persons," in *The Handbook of Interethnic Coexistence* (New York: Continuum, 1998).

For expatriate children, tolerance is not a luxury but a necessity. They must be able to get along with others who are different. In international schools, children who are unable to do so can become isolated because the majority of the other children are from all over the world. Children who can accept different others are also better at accepting themselves when *they* are the ones who are different. Abroad, it is our children who are different. They are the foreigners.

However, tolerance is not instinctive. Fear and uncertainty are more common reactions to a foreign environment. We often develop stereotypes about the cultures we come into contact with. And most expatriates react angrily to the frustrations of living in a foreign country, sometimes criticizing or becoming hostile toward the host culture. The stress of living in close contact with other cultures can make us less tolerant rather than more so. We therefore must make even more of an effort to be tolerant.

> Seven-year-old Rory had grown up in three foreign countries. Shortly after starting school in his own country, he came home upset. "The other kids said my sandals are stupid." "Do you want to get some the same?" his mother asked. "No," said Rory, "I like these, but why did they laugh? Why does everyone have to wear the same?"

Expatriate children have a head start on tolerance. They are used to situations in which everyone is different. They also go through fads, and some national groups insist on high levels of conformity. In general, however, they accept a wide range of differences.

> Steve says, " We think tolerance is important. We avoid ethnic jokes or being negative about Korea. Our friends are from all over the world and we've tried to learn different languages—if not very diligently. I really thought we were teaching our kids tolerance. But one day Davie—he's 14—yelled at me: 'You're always talking about tolerance but you hate my music, my hair, my posters. Whatever I like, you think is stupid.' I was shocked, but in a way he was right."

If we wish to teach our children tolerance, it must be valued and practiced at home, in mundane interactions as well as discussions. When we accept and respect our children and listen to them, taking their problems and ideas seriously, we both model tolerance and promote a positive self-image. Children with high self-esteem are better able to be tolerant of others.

Dealing with Prejudice and Intolerance

Our children will also be confronted with intolerance and prejudice. Peers at school will say hurtful things about our country, religion, or culture. Their friends' parents will consider our children rude because they don't remove their shoes at the door or observe the courtesies *they* consider natural and necessary. Host-country nationals demonstrate various prejudices.

> Twenty-year-old Nancy occasionally eats meat, but she says, "I still feel guilty. I was a vegetarian for six years. I started because my friends in New Delhi were Hindus, and if I took meat for lunch, they wouldn't sit with me. They made fun of me for talking about saving the whale but still eating meat."

Intolerance hurts. Children have difficulty with the anger or pain caused by misconceptions or prejudice, particularly when friends have hurt them. This anger tends to be "passed on." Children who have been hurt are more likely to hurt others. However, if handled correctly such incidents can help children learn to deal with their emotions as well as with the pain prejudice causes. They can learn to avoid being intolerant and prejudiced themselves.

> Thirteen-year-old Jacob sat alone in the cafeteria at his new school every day for two weeks until teachers realized that he was being boycotted because he was an Israeli. They intervened, but not before the boy had gone through a traumatic ordeal.

Children cannot cope with extreme prejudice. If they are told every day that they are stupid, undesirable, wicked, or whatever, children will come to see themselves in this light. In an international environment, children often make each other responsible for their country or ethnic or religious group. Although there is an important difference between accidental injury and deliberate insult, if a child is being regularly injured by cultural or national prejudice, contact the school administrators immediately. Ask what steps they plan to take. If the situation does not change, take your child out of the situation, permanently if necessary.

Turning Prejudice Around

Children can be mean and vicious, but they can also be tolerant and kind. Schools can create a climate of tolerance, helping both students and teachers deal with the misunderstandings and conflicts that inevitably arise when so many cultures come together. Support programs designed to promote tolerance, and encourage schools to be proactive in countering prejudice.

> Zak, an 8-year-old Greek-American boy, was playing football with the neighborhood children in Cyprus when his mother heard the other children making fun of the "xenos," foreigner. Taking some cookies with her, she went out to offer them around and spent a few minutes chatting and getting to know the children.

Take positive steps to break through prejudice. It is harder to keep up negative stereotypes about other countries when we have friends from those countries. Get to know your neighbors. Introduce yourself to the parents of your children's friends. We are all more understanding with the children of our friends. Share the good things about your country and culture. Invite your children's friends to join in special meals or celebrations.

To promote tolerance and help children deal with intolerance:

- *Promote self-esteem.* Children need encouragement, kindness, and tolerance if they are to grow up feeling

confident enough to avoid being intolerant and to
face prejudice.

- *Encourage and model empathy.* Children who can empa-
thize with others are less likely to treat them badly.
Demonstrate empathy when your child is sad or hurt.
Talk about other people's feelings: "I think Ingrid must
be feeling sad because her friend has left."
- *Promote and model flexibility in thinking.* Living with
culturally different people requires accepting that
different ideas can exist at the same time as well as
being able to take different perspectives. Engage in
open dialogue with your children. Discuss different
behaviors.
- *Talk about hurtful incidents.* Help children identify and
accept their sadness, anger, and frustration and that of
others when confronted with prejudice.
- *Discuss how to avoid hurtful situations.* What misconceptions, comments, or jokes hurt your children? What
upsets their friends?
- *Practice strategies.* How can cultural misconceptions be
corrected? What is the best way for children to tell a
friend that they feel hurt? How can they apologize
when they hurt someone? When should they seek help
from adults?

Ethical and Religious Education

Dialogue can help us recognize that other faiths than our
own are genuine mansions of the spirit.
——*Archbishop of Canterbury, 1986*

*We often have closer contact with people of other religions abroad
than at home,* where most people belong to the majority religion and every religion has an established place. Abroad, the
majority religion may be quite different, confronting us daily
with another religion and the cultural mores derived from it.
Our expatriate friends and those of our children also frequently are of other faiths.

Expatriate children are more likely to question their own faith. With friends from different religions, children quite naturally wonder why they learn different things. Take this opportunity to discuss why you believe what you do; open a dialogue about your faith, ethics, and values. This promotes children's understanding of these issues, as well as of their own religion.

Many expatriates do not have a formal religion or do not practice their religion. As a result, there is no natural forum in which to discuss beliefs and ethics with children. The principles they live by are not set down in a book or formulated as a set of teachings. In this case, make a special effort to convey your principles to your children. For instance, why don't you steal? When you tell your children that they should respect others, what exactly do you mean? Help your children formulate a reply to the question, "What religion are you?" In some countries religion is an important marker. In Saudi Arabia, for instance, if you indicate that you are atheist or agnostic, you will be denied entry to the country. In many ways, questions about religion are also questions about culture, because many aspects of culture are closely related to the main religion in a country.

Religion is the hardest thing to be tolerant about. Complete religious tolerance would mean accepting all religions as equal, something almost none of us can do. Instead, we can use the concept of religious acceptance, accepting other people's right to have different beliefs without accepting the beliefs themselves. To be a good Muslim is right for a Muslim child. To be a good Christian is right for a Christian child. Children can usually accept this type of reasoning without difficulty. After all, their friends are different from them in so many other ways as well.

The meeting of religions creates practical challenges. Children may be invited to participate in other children's religious observances or celebrations, for instance. Learning about other faiths is a valuable experience for children, but make sure that these situations are used to promote understanding and nothing more. Trying to convert children is unethical, but people are sometimes carried away by their convictions. If you are concerned about what other parents are telling your children, express your concern. "I know that you would like my child to understand your religion, but our child is...and we believe that..."

Expatriates get to know typical members of a religion. At home, our impressions of other religions often come from the media, which pays attention primarily when there is conflict. Expatriates come into contact with the average members of various religions and therefore have an opportunity to gain a more balanced view of other religions.

> Jim says, "Our daughter was only 7, but other kids in her class would tell her that America was evil. We spoke to the school about it, but they said it was very difficult to deal with, because that's what the religious leaders were saying."

Religious acceptance is not always a two-way street. Encourage children to accept their friends' religions, but emphasize that they have a right to their own religion. This is difficult in countries where other religions are banned or where children encounter religious prejudice. Discuss these issues with your children. Help them develop strategies for correcting misconceptions. Use the effects of intolerance to explain why you support religious tolerance.

To provide ethical or religious guidance:

- *Welcome contact with other religions.* Children's questions about other people's religions provide an ideal opportunity to explain why you hold the religious or ethical values you do. Encourage your children to understand other religions, but protect them from attempts at conversion.
- *Communicate ethical values.* If you do not have an established religion, take extra care to communicate important beliefs and values to your children. Help them decide what to reply when asked about their religion.

- *Help your children develop strategies* to confront religious intolerance, such as correcting misconceptions or expressing hurt when confronted with intolerance. Use the effects of intolerance to explain why you support religious tolerance.

Chapter 14
Identity

Nineteen-year-old Jason says, "When people ask me where I'm from, I don't know what to say. I mean, I have an American passport, but I never lived here until now. If I say I'm from North Carolina, where my Mom and Dad are from, people make comments about the Panthers or something and I can't really say anything intelligent. I can't say I'm from Rome, even though that's the place that still feels most like home, or that I was born in Singapore. I just don't look the part somehow."

"*Where am I from?*" and "*Who am I?*" are questions with a special twist for expatriate children. When people ask where you are from, they're asking not just about a geographic place, but about the country and culture you feel you belong to. Expatriate children who have spent years outside their own country often feel that stating their nationality does not answer the question, not only for others but for themselves. They feel that there must be something wrong because they don't have an easy answer.

Ironically, it is often the questions rather than their lives that cause problems. Many expatriate children have a healthy sense of themselves. They don't feel that they're from nowhere; rather, they feel that they are from many places. They also have strong ties to a wide circle of friends, even though they may be scattered around the world, as well as to family. Several things in the expatriate environment may actually promote a healthy sense of self. The need for different perspectives can be good training for coping with the "multiple selves" of adolescence. Being confronted with many cultures pushes children into making choices about how to behave and what to think. Also, moving forces children to develop a sense of themselves, away from friends and support groups.

However, there are special challenges for expatriate children. Because they have contact with different countries and cultures, they have many choices in deciding who they are and where they belong. Many have lived in several countries. They may even have more than one nationality and passport, either because their parents are from different countries or because they acquired citizenship while residing in a country. But regardless of where children have legal rights, they often feel that they "belong" in some way to the countries they have lived in, and each country influences them in some way. Expatriate children absorb facets of other cultures and mindsets. They are influenced by friends from many countries. All of these elements must eventually be reconciled into a coherent sense of self.

The Meaning of Identity

Simply put, identity is who we feel we are. Because humans are social creatures, it is also what other people think of us. "Me" is a mixture of personal characteristics and our relationships to various social groups. These groups usually include family, people of the same nationality, and those with whom we have something in common—computer wizards, for instance, or those who believe in protecting the environment. People with a healthy identity have synthesised a coherent identity out of these elements. A healthy identity also continues to develop throughout life. Our view of ourselves changes as we move from adolescence through adulthood.

Identity Development

> Linda and John had been living in a village in New Guinea for several years. Preparing to attend a friend's wedding, Linda had a lot of trouble persuading her son to put on shoes instead of going barefoot or wearing his scuffed sandals. Next day the 4-year-old came to her and said, "Mommy, can I be brown when I grow up so I can be barefoot?" It took Linda a moment to realize that because most of the adults in the village went barefoot, her son had assumed that if his skin was brown he would not have to wear shoes.

The development of a self-concept is a long process that begins around age 2, when children discover themselves as individuals separate from their parents. Children begin by recognizing their physical features, first in isolation ("I am a good football player"), then in relation to others ("I am a better football player than Tom"). It takes time for children to grasp the nature of identity and the permanence of certain physical features. Their understanding of the relationship between themselves and the world, including the concept of belonging to groups, develops gradually. As a result, young children often cannot relate to nationality, and "Where are you from" is interpreted as "Where do you live?" If this happens, accept whatever answer your children give. Don't make them feel as if they have given the wrong answer, but explain that they are also from somewhere else. Talk about your home country, their grandparents, or other things they can relate to. Encourage them to consider having more than one home an advantage.

In middle childhood, groups become part of children's picture of themselves: "I'm on the Tigers baseball team," "I'm a Boy

Scout." Self-descriptions begin to include personal attributes: "I am kind," "I'm scared of heights." These become progressively less concrete. Teenagers often use more complex and global attributes — "I am tolerant" or "I believe in protecting the environment." Eventually all these features are incorporated into the young adult's self-image.

Stages of personal identification:

- *Physical descriptions.* Hair and eye color.
- *Group membership.* I am a Boy Scout, class president, football player.
- *Personality.* I am patient, kind, generous.
- *Global concepts.* I am a member of the human race. I believe in equality.

> My kids never used to mention their friends' ethnic group. I knew their names and things about them — that one was the best reader in the class, for instance, or that another always wore pretty hair clasps — but when the kids came over for a birthday party, I never had a picture of them in my mind.

Children become aware of ethnic differences when they are 3 or 4 years old, and when they are between 4 and 8 years old they can recognize their own ethnic group. While there is no reason to think that expatriate children develop differently than others, it is possible that ethnic groups have less significance for them. In a group of twenty expatriate children, there may be fourteen or fifteen nationalities, with few of the socioeconomic differences or negative social stereotypes that make ethnic differences significant. However, children living in countries in which foreigners are particularly unwelcome may become even more aware of their ethnic origin — which may affect their self-esteem, particularly if they are physically identifiable as foreigners.

Identity Integration

A major task for adolescents is to develop an integrated personal identity, a sense of who they are and who they want to become, as well as their place in the world. These processes are often more complex for expatriate children. Because of their experiences, they have more options. Even something like "I want to be an honest person," for instance, is not a straightforward decision, since honesty means different things in different cultures. Children who have experienced these differences must decide what they mean by honesty. Deciding on their place in the world is equally complex, and most expatriate children don't have easy answers. At this point in history, nationality is fundamental to people's identity, but many expatriate children feel that they belong in various ways to other countries as well. Others may not have strong feelings about their own nationality.

Expatriate children are exposed to many perspectives, making it difficult for them to decide what to think. Young adolescents in particular are just learning to weigh what they think about issues against what others think, and they may be overwhelmed by pressure from all sides. Their parents, for instance, may think that cheating at school is highly unethical, while some of their friends may believe that cheating is just a way for friends to help each other, or even that cheating is a game. Other friends may feel obligated to report those who cheat. What stand should teenagers take on this issue? How should they respond to each of their friends? Ultimately, many expatriate children learn to make very mature decisions, but young adolescents — and their parents — often find the learning process challenging.

Adolescent expatriates may be confused by other people's definitions of them. An important part of our identity is defined by our relationship to our social environment, but expatriate teenagers are exposed to conflicting sets of expectations. In the host country, people judge them according to one set of standards, teachers at school according to another very different one, and people at home in yet another way. This can cause some teenagers to feel threatened when others attempt to define them in a way that they feel is not accurate — even when they themselves are not yet sure what is accurate. Sometimes they resent it when we talk about them, even in a straightforward manner — "Bryan is an adventurous young lad"; "Sarah does well at school," for instance. Listen carefully when teenagers tell you about themselves or what they like. They are often "trying out" an aspect of their identity. Discuss their alternatives with them, but accept their perceptions of themselves.

> Twenty-year-old Roberta says, "I just wish everybody here would get over their identity crises. They are all still so concerned about what their friends think. They really haven't cut the umbilical cord yet and can't exist on their own. If I'd been like that, I'd never have survived abroad. Sometimes I don't hear from my friends for six months, but I don't curl up and die in the meantime."

Expatriate children often learn to exist independently relatively early. In a new place they are always alone for a while, a painful experience, but they learn that they can survive and eventually make new friends. Group pressure also has natural limits. A group of girls from Indonesia, New Zealand, Cyprus, and the United States, for instance, simply cannot be the same. This does not mean that expatriate children are not subject to group pressures, but there is often more freedom—and need—to be different and to develop personal attitudes. However, some children are overwhelmed by the complexity of their situation. A few simplify matters by becoming extremely nationalistic or seeking black-and-white answers: "This is right and that is wrong." Others have difficulty synthesizing the many options they have. They may vacillate and avoid making decisions and judgments, or try out many different identity options.

Cultural Differences

There are cultural differences in identity development, particularly in the balance between individualism and responsiveness to social groups. Individualistic cultures such as those of North America, Australasia, and much of Europe emphasize "thinking for yourself" and self-sufficiency. Relational cultures, which include those of much of Asia, South America, the Mediterranean, the Middle East, and Africa, put more weight on sensitivity to social groups. Although expatriate children do not reflect their own cultures in the same way that they would if they were growing up at home, children from different cultural groups still experience different problems. Children from relational cultures may find that their friends don't understand their sensitivity to pressures from family or fellow nationals. At the same time, because they have adapted to the culture of international schools or friends from other cultures, their parents may consider them rebellious compared to children at home. Children from individualistic cultures may find that friends from relational cultures find them egotistical and insensitive to the obligations of friendship.

Social Identities

The groups that we feel we belong to are an important part of our identity. A sense of self is a mosaic not just of personal characteristics but also of the social groups we belong to. Children learn to become part of social communities by belonging to groups. They learn to relate to others and develop feelings of caring and empathy through belonging. Without these feelings, there is no pressure to behave in socially acceptable ways. In the expatriate situation, children's relationships to some social groups are disrupted. Children grow up outside their own culture. They join groups such as sports teams or other activity groups and then have to move on. Friendships are interrupted. One study has indicated that later in life some expatriate children feel comfortable in many environments but often don't feel part of any one.* But expatriate children do not need to miss out on the experience of belonging or of social commitment and responsibility.

We can promote children's social relationships by encouraging them to join groups and maintain long-term commitments where possible. Family and national memberships are

---

* Downie, R. *Reentry Experiences and Identity Formation for Third Culture Experiences of Dependent Youth: An Exploratory Study.* Ph.D. Thesis, Michigan State University, East Lansing, MI. 1976.

enduring social relationships, and we can also foster commitment to school, expatriate, local, and global communities as well as sports and other activity groups. We can do this by helping our children establish connections and keep up relationships, providing logistical support, and encouraging commitment and responsibility. We also teach by example, through our own contributions to various groups.

National Identity

> Shalwa, the mother of three children, says, "I never know what my children are going to say when someone asks them where they are from. They have dual citizenship and have grown up abroad. One child might say she's Jordanian or Egyptian, since she was born there. Our oldest usually says he's Canadian. The little one sometimes says he is from Cyprus, or he comes and asks me what to say. For the two older ones, though, it depends a bit on the political situation or who asks them.

Abroad, children's relationship to a national group often causes them concern. They are constantly being asked "Where are you from?" and struggling to find an answer that satisfies people but also expresses how they feel. Returning home can also cause problems. Having been raised to think of themselves as American, Indian, Colombian, Russian, or whatever, children may find that they don't have much in common with their fellow nationals. It is also largely nationality, or at least a geographic place, that people have in mind when they talk about feeling rootless.

> "I can say I'm British, can't I, Daddy?" Anna asked. "We lived there for a while and all the other kids I like are from there."

Children are sometimes not sure which countries they are "allowed" to belong to, or they may switch allegiances. It can suddenly become an advantage to be French, for example, if France has just won the World Cup. In other situations an identity may be denied because it has acquired a negative value. A country may become unpopular for political reasons or because friends ridicule it. Sometimes children just want to try out different countries, or they want to belong to a specific national group because their friends do. Accept your children's choices, but help them learn to appreciate their country(ies) independently of other people's concepts. If they are sports fans, find out who has excelled at some sport in your country. If they have an interest in music, help them discover some of their national melodies.

> Regine, a middle-school teacher, says, "I really liked my seventh-grade social studies class. Most of the kids had been friends for years. They had gone to each other's birthday parties and slept at each other's homes without worrying about race or nationality, but toward the end of last year things started to change. John's best friend stopped spending time with him because he preferred to be with the group of Arab boys. Antie, a Finnish boy, started hanging out with the three Russian boys in the class. Several of the kids were kind of left in the middle. I felt really sad."

Preadolescents and early adolescents often experience national or ethnic identity in a new way. They want to explore the meaning of this part of their identity, and it can suddenly become very important. They become aware of concepts of loyalty and patriotism. As a result, in international schools this can be a time when there is more cross-cultural conflict than at other ages. Many expatriate children, with parents who are diplomats, members of international organizations, or international businesspeople, are also politically more aware than peers at home.

> Ian says, "When people at home start talking about 'Africa,' I often get angry. For a start, it is a whole continent with heaps of different countries. And when they start on the conflicts and wars there, they are bound to make some comment about it being primitive—as if there are no wars anywhere else or we don't have a hand in those wars. But I never know what to say. Where do you start?"

*In late adolescence many expatriate children develop mature po-
litical stances.* Because of their personal contact with people from
other countries, they are aware that countries and cultures are
complex, and they do not readily accept simplistic stereotypes.
This sometimes puts them in an awkward position, particularly when their country is in conflict with another country, but
they can't agree with the rhetoric of the day.

> While Dana was packing to leave Berlin for the two-month
> summer break, her 14-year-old, sprawled on the bed, said,
> "I'm going to get as much American culture as I can when
> I'm home." "What exactly are you planning to do?" Dana
> asked. "I'm going to eat at Burger King and watch sitcoms,"
> her daughter replied. Ten minutes later Dana's 17-year-old
> daughter, Sara, asked, "Mom, what do you do if you don't
> like your own culture?"

*Expatriate children sometimes develop stereotypical pictures of their
country.* Often their contact with it has been limited, or they
have forgotten a lot and pick up ideas from brief visits, TV, or
what other people say. As a result, they judge their home country the way foreigners would. Parents can help children develop
a more differentiated picture of their home country. As they
grow older, discuss more and more complex issues with them —
things that happen there, problems and innovations. This helps
children see their country more realistically.

To promote a national identity:

- *Celebrate national holidays and events.*
- *Help your children gain knowledge about their country(ies).*
  Growing up in one country, we absorb a lot of general
  knowledge about it. Our children do not have the same
  opportunities. Help them discover their country
  through trips, books, personal stories, videos, and
  games. Encourage them to recognize the complexity of
  a national identity rather than a set of stereotypes or
  symbols.

- *Participate in a national club if there is one,* but don't isolate yourself from others.

Family

The family is one of children's primary groups. It is also the most continuous social group in the lives of expatriate children, the only people who have shared their experiences through various postings. Parents and siblings are the keepers of children's personal histories: "Look, this photo shows you at the beach in Bahrain," "Do you remember that horrible math teacher in Kinshasa?" These pictures of their lives help children develop a healthy identity, which must incorporate the past as well as a vision of the future.

To promote a family identity:

- *Keep up family traditions or create new ones.* Improvise if necessary.
- *Mark significant events*—the first day at a new school, the last night in a house.
- *Share family history*—stories about parents' or grandparents' lives, for instance.
- *Make personal timelines, journals, or photo albums* to give your children a sense of their own history. Talk about events and incidents in their lives.

Other Communities

There are many groups or communities to which expatriate children can belong. Foster participation in such groups. In this way children's experiences abroad will be richer and they will learn the skills they need to participate in groups. Children learn by example, so we should become involved ourselves. Parents can volunteer to help at school or in expatriate organizations. We can get to know local people or get involved in local groups. Taking an interest in local issues, even through English-language newspapers, demonstrates commitment to our present environment. Equally, an interest in international affairs or involvement in an international organization shows commitment to the global community.

Children naturally become part of school communities, but levels of involvement vary. Encourage your children to participate in various ways—in extracurricular activities or student politics, for instance. Mobile activities and interests also help children join social groups in each new place. Children who play musical instruments can become part of the orchestra at school or in the local community. Those who play a sport can join teams. Bird watchers, stamp collectors, or chess players will find like-minded people the world over. Be prepared to provide logistical support for children, such as driving them to and from school activities.

Expatriates are often isolated from the local community. International schools frequently try to forge links to local communities, but parents can also help. If there are no language barriers, children can participate in local groups: playing on local sports teams, helping to raise funds for charities, participating in local activities or celebrations. Children will feel more connected to a local community if their parents also have local friends, take an interest in local events and affairs, and are prepared to contribute to the local community in some way.

Expatriate children belong to global communities. After a few years abroad, they may have friends from all over the world. We can also help them take on global responsibilities by discussing world issues with them and encouraging them to participate in international organizations such as Amnesty International or the Red Cross.

To promote other-group or community identities:

- *Encourage participation in groups and communities.*
  Children must learn the social skills that enable them to be part of a group or community.
- *Encourage your children to develop "mobile" interests.*
  Interests and activities that children can practice anywhere or that help them become part of a group in different places are an advantage.
- *Set a good example* through your own interest and participation in groups.

Promoting Healthy Identity Development

Parents can promote healthy identity development. Although a child's identity mosaic is not really put together until adolescence, the roots are laid down much earlier. We can encourage children to explore and become aware of all aspects of their identity in ways appropriate to their ages. Encourage them to learn about their various countries, including the home country and others they have lived in. Offer encouragement and logistical help so that they can maintain contact with social groups, whether friends or national groups. Discussions help children consider their options and make rational decisions.

Promoting identity in early and middle childhood:

- *Explore physical characteristics* such as eye and hair color, height, weight, and thumb prints.
- *Explore personal characteristics* such as personal traits, likes and dislikes, abilities and interests; use self-portraits, collages, and so forth.
- *Promote a sense of self and personal history.* Help your children develop a sense of their lives. Keep photo albums, journals, or a record of funny things said, people who were part of their lives, and the like. If they are too small to write themselves, let them dictate stories to you or draw pictures. Draw a family tree and tell stories from your life.

Preadolescents and Adolescents

For expatriate adolescents the identity-building process can be painful. They must integrate many pieces to integrate into their self-concept. Helping adolescents work through their identity crises is also challenging for parents. Adolescents try out different ideas and behaviors. Although many of these experiments are short-lived, our children inevitably make some choices that we don't like. They can also be difficult to live with. When they are confused or unhappy, they may be grumpy and moody. However, we can help them work through their choices. Discussing issues openly gives them the opportunity to talk things through as well as helping them develop skills in rational thinking. If we listen, we can understand them better and can sometimes guide them.

Promoting identity in preadolescents and adolescents:

- *Encourage exploration.* Teenagers must try out various activities, fashions, music, and so forth, as well as social situations.
- *Allow your children to make decisions* so that they can learn to make responsible decisions. Practice makes perfect.
- *Encourage activities that explore a sense of self,* such as keeping a journal or diary, writing letters and e-mails, or creating family trees.
- *Encourage integration activities* such as self-portraiture or assignments using personal experiences.
- *Discuss issues.* Allow your children to express ideas and explore a variety of perspectives.
- *Promote participation* in various groups. Encourage your children to seek groups that they can relate to, keep up with old friends, and find enduring social groups.
- *Support future plans.* Encourage your children to think about what they want to do and consider a variety of options.

Chapter 15
Expatriate Children

Sonja says, "Melissa's studying medicine. She decided that was what she wanted to do when we were living in Bangladesh. I think it was seeing all the misery there. I guess she felt that she wanted to be able to do something about it. It's quite a financial burden. We've got two other kids as well, and her Dad jokes that then she'll probably go off and work for Doctors Without Borders or something and we'll still be supporting her. I mean, that's fine and we're proud of her, but that would be a really hard life."

When children live abroad, the courses of their lives are changed. But what is it that changes? In what way are they different from their peers? How will their futures be affected? Most grown-up expatriate children believe that living abroad has affected their lives, from career choices to how they relate to others. Many feel different from their peers. When we take children to other countries, we take on a special responsibility.

To understand the implications of our choices, we must look at the effects of living abroad on children.

> Nineteen-year-old David says, "We're all individuals, not just a big mass of TCKs (third culture kids). I wish people would remember that."

We talk about expatriate children collectively, but they come from every country in the world. Each has lived in different countries and has had a unique set of experiences. Almost all feel that they are different from others, whether at home or abroad. However, many of their experiences are similar, from international moves to international schooling. Certain issues are relevant to all expatriate children — for example, the effects of moving and growing up in other cultures and of fitting in back home again.

> Twenty-one-year-old Kate says, "It's only when you go back home and compare your experiences with others that you realize how much more interesting your life has been and how much more interesting it will be because you 'see' so much more."

Many expatriate children are glad that they have lived abroad and feel that their lives have been richer, more interesting as a result, but they also feel that they have paid a price. They may never quite fit in at home, for instance, or may feel that they have missed out on things like high school athletic programs or staying in one place long enough to become good at an activity. Some are affected in more serious ways: They are plagued by feelings of homelessness, unresolved grief, and loneliness. In terms of education, most expatriate children are quite successful. According to a large U.S. study, nearly 90 percent of adult expatriate children have some academic postsecondary education, and more than 40 percent have earned a graduate degree. Over 80 percent have become professionals, semiprofessionals, managers or officials.[*]

---

[*] Cottrell, A. Baker, J. and R. Hill Useem, and K. Finn Jordan. "Third Culture Kids: Focus of Major Study," *Newslinks, Newspaper of the*

Farah says, "It's all in how you see it, really. There's just
about nothing that doesn't have a flip side. Going new places
is horrible in some ways, but you learn how to survive on
your own and how to make friends. You have to prove yourself all over again as well, but you also get a new chance. No
one is saying, 'Well, she's like this or that.' I just happen to be
really positive, so I think I got the best out of it."

Children's experiences of the same situations are different. How
they feel about the advantages or the difficulties and challenges of expatriate life depends to some extent on their ability to see things in a positive or a negative light, both while
they lived abroad and as adults back home. Those who see life
abroad as an opportunity often suffer less when confronted by
difficulties and challenges. Those who are able to consider their
international background in a positive light as adults are better able to utilize the skills they acquired.

A third culture kid (TCK) is a person who has spent a significant part of his or her developmental years outside the
parents' culture.*

Expatriate children are often referred to as third culture kids (TCKs).
This expression is not used here because of the difficulty
of deciding what comprises a significant part of children's
developmental years. Many of the challenges of parenting
are the same no matter how long a family spends abroad.
Some children who are not technically TCKs are confronted
with similar advantages and challenges—bicultural children or those attending international schools, for instance.
The concept, developed by Ruth Hill Useem in the 1950s,
refers to the lifestyle these children share within the expatriate community. In this sense it includes all of these
children, since most participate in expatriate communities in one way or another.

International Schools Services, January 1993, p. 1; 680 adult third
culture kids (ATCKs) between the ages of 25 and 84 participated in
the study.
* *The TCK Profile,* 1989, as cited by David C. Pollock and Ruth E. Van
Reken, 1999, p. 35.

Traits of Expatriate Children

What have I gained, what have I lost...? My wisdom has flourished in Rome, my passion in Cairo, my anguish in Fez, and my innocence still flourishes in Granada. ——*Amin Maalouf**

Expatriate children are unique individuals, yet they are the same. Because of their unique backgrounds, they are a diverse group of individuals. At the same time, most have shared a similar lifestyle. They have been part of the expatriate community — the so-called third culture—and have faced similar challenges. As a result, they share some common traits.

Adaptability

Shannon says, "It's a shame when you can't keep up with the things you like doing. On the other hand, you learn to jump in and just do things: 'Okay, teach me how and I'll play.' You kind of have to eat humble pie all the time. That's hard, especially if you're a teenager and most of the time no one else is doing it."

Adaptability is the most characteristic trait of expatriate children. To survive abroad they learn to be adaptable on many levels, from the purely physical ones of learning their way around a new city to fitting into new social groups. Adjusting to different situations is challenging, but rising to meet these challenges is an opportunity for personal growth.

Marya says, "Moving's tough, but in a way having your boat rocked is good for you. You get ahead in personal growth. When I look at friends here, they're great, but they're kind of immature."

Many expatriate children discover that they are different from their peers, not only because they have been places and done things that others haven't, but because they have also developed

* Maalouf, Amin. *Leo the African* (Abacus, 1994).

faster than others on a personal level, confronting cross-
cultural or political issues, or questioning who they are. The
challenges of expatriate friendships have taught them many
complex social skills. However, even "positive" differences
can make them feel out of step with others. And some expatriate children are less, rather than more, mature than their
peers. Those who have moved often may not have grasped
some of the essentials of maintaining social relationships.
Some were overwhelmed by the diversity they experienced
and failed to find an appropriate balance between personal
needs and social demands, dependence and independence,
or various cultural mores.

Internationalism

*Many expatriate children continue to feel "international" long af-
ter returning home.* Their perspectives continue to be different
from those of their peers—more differentiated and defined less
in terms of black and white, "We are right and they are wrong,"
although they may become less so in time. Many retain a height-
ened interest in world affairs or previous host countries. Some
seek jobs in international corporations and organizations. However, many feel that they don't have the opportunity to use their
international skills as much as they would like to.

> Hugo says, "We sent David back to a university in Vancouver,
> partly so he would get to know other Canadians, but he seems
> to spend all his time with people from other countries. His
> girlfriend right now is from Geneva."

*Expatriate children often feel that they have more in common with
one another than with peers at home.* In some cases they are able
to share their experiences through groups of other expatriate children such as Global Nomads.* Many maintain contact with friends around the world, although this may be

---

* Global Nomads International (GNI) is a nonprofit organization
that provides a forum for expatriate children of all ages to share
experiences and information. It is based in the United States, but
its members come from all over the world.

sporadic. In college, they gravitate toward international groups or seek friendships with people from other countries. Unfortunately, in some cases this occurs at the expense of finding home-country friends.

Creativity

> Creativity is not only concerned with generating new ideas, but with escaping old ones. —— *Edward de Bono.**

Expatriate children learn to think creatively. As young children abroad, they do not have old ideas to escape from before they can absorb new ones. As adults, they don't need to learn that there are different ways of classifying knowledge or organizing concepts and systems. Other systems have already been absorbed and accommodated into the way they think. Contact with other systems of thought at an age when the brain is still capable of change leaves children with these constructs as part of their basic system of analysis.

> Wendy, a fifth-grade teacher, says, "When the kids write stories, you can sometimes tell where they have lived. They take pieces from everywhere for inspiration. One girl wrote about a jungle taking over the city (Nicosia). You could tell that she really knew the jungle—the mass of twisting trees and vines and so on."

Abroad, even young children are confronted with problem-solving situations, such as how to communicate with people who speak different languages, or what teachers in various schools expect in terms of courtesy. Children learn that there is more than one solution to most problems and more than one appropriate behavior in many situations. Their experiences with other people and in other countries provide them with a mental "library" of options when seeking solutions or innovative ideas.

---

* De Bono, Edward. *Lateral Thinking for Management.* London: Penguin Books, 1971, p. 2.

Social Orientation, Tolerance

Empathy is not just feeling for *someone but feeling* with *them.*
Expatriate children spend at least part of their lives walking,
if not in others' shoes, then alongside them. They accept friends'
differences and strive to understand other ways of thinking
and behaving. Many expatriate children feel that they can
communicate with many kinds of people and handle a wide
variety of social situations. Many find themselves mediating
for others or helping to bridge communication gaps.

*As adults, many expatriate children demonstrate social commit-
ment.* This may be because in foreign environments expatriates
expect to provide support for one another, whether it involves
showing a newcomer where to shop or helping out in a crisis.
Friendships are often intense, both because expatriates often
share difficult times and because there is always the chance that
one or the other person will have to leave soon. However, some
children, having moved often, find it difficult to make a commitment, either to individuals or to groups.

Issues

*Adults who have grown up abroad carry their traveling childhoods
with them.* They must come to terms with the long-term effects of mobility, sometimes having difficulty settling in one
place or, alternatively, never wanting to move again. Mobility influences children's social development, affecting their
adult relationships in the context of friendships, partnerships,
and community relationships.

Mobility

Thirty-year-old Samantha, the daughter of a diplomat, spent
her life moving around the world until she was sent to boarding school at the age of 14. After finishing school she contin-
ued to travel, working as a freelance journalist and

photographer. She stopped only five years ago, when she married a Greek man and settled in Athens. Like her four siblings, she has been disinherited by her father, who finds all his children to be lacking in seriousness and stability.

Mobility is a two-edged sword. Children who move often learn to be adaptable and to cope with change, but mobility is also potentially the most destructive aspect of the international lifestyle. The pain of leaving friends, schools, and activities every couple of years, along with the challenges of starting over, has short-term and long-term consequences, from schooling deficits to difficulty settling down. The grief experienced when leaving friends can become a constant companion of adult expatriates, affecting their relationships. The loneliness and embarrassment of being new or an outsider can affect their self-esteem.

> Kay attended three universities before she earned her bachelor's degree. In the five years that followed, she changed jobs three times, moving from one end of the country to the other. Then she married and settled in Geneva with her Swiss spouse. She says, "At the moment it's a challenge, but I wonder what will happen when the novelty wears off. That's usually when I start to think about moving on."

Expatriate children may remain mobile all their lives. Particularly those who have moved often seem to develop an inner program that every few years tells them it is time to move on again. And moving is relatively easy. They are not inhibited by strong ties to any one place or discouraged by the problems of moving somewhere new. For some, moving is simply the only life they have known, and they enjoy the constant challenge and stimulation of new places. Others like the "tabula rasa" effect, the chance to start anew in each place, both in friendships and in the way they live their lives. Others react in the opposite way: When they finally settle down, they never want to move again. Or they may feel that they have already seen enough of the world.

Friendships

> Sharifa says, "It's embarrassing. Every time I go to an air-
> port I start crying even if no one is leaving. I still can't bear
> it when people leave, or when I have to."

*Most expatriate children say that leaving friends is the worst thing
about moving.* And making new friends is the most difficult
thing. Most never forget what it is like to be the only one
who doesn't know anyone else. But those who have moved
often know that they *will* make friends eventually. Most learn
to make friends relatively quickly, to approach others and
accept invitations. Friendships often develop differently than
at home. Perhaps because of the experience of being together
in a foreign country, relationships can be intense, often taking the place of extended family. With the constant threat of
leaving, relationships tend to develop quickly.

*Expatriate children sometimes have different expectations of friend-
ships than do people at home.* As a result, they may be disappointed when people at home are not as committed to their
friendships or don't immediately enter into intense relationships. Their friendships are also inhibited by the inability of
friends at home to share their overseas experiences.

> Faith's "My Life" albums of photos, mementos, and stories
> have helped her share her past with close friends, several of
> whom have read them from cover to cover.

*Some friends at home will make the effort to understand expatriate
children—in time.* It is easier if the situation is one of mutual
exchange. "Teach me about living here, and I can tell you about
Algiers or Buenos Aires." Although expatriate children often
feel different from those at home, this is not always perceived
as an isolating factor. Abroad, many friends were also quite different, yet close relationships were still possible.

> I thought it would be hard to get used to being back in
> Australia and that the others maybe wouldn't like me, but
> everyone wanted to be with me. I think it was because I

treated everyone as an individual, and with me they could be whatever they wanted. With each other, they had to behave a certain way. They'd all known each other so long that they assumed things about each other that weren't necessarily true anymore.

Many expatriate children learn to accept other people as individuals. Children in international schools are so different in terms of nationality, culture, and background that they have to accept others as they are. This is a useful skill even when they return home. However, it tends to be more of an asset in college than in high school. At this age, efforts to be different become stronger than social pressure to be the same.

Partnerships

Toby grew up in Iowa. He has little facility for languages and is not comfortable with people from other cultures. Sarah has lived all over the world and planned a career abroad, but she knows that she may eventually have to choose between Toby and the lifestyle she always visualized for herself.

Expatriate children rarely find someone from the same "culture." They have grown up amid a mixture of cultural influences, and even in their home country their peers are different. Every relationship will be cross-cultural in some ways.

As a child, Rohan lived in seven different countries, returning to New Zealand only to attend college. Today he lives in Christchurch and is quite happy where he is for the moment. "I'll probably go somewhere eventually, but I'm not in a hurry. I've already been to so many places." His wife, however, is anxious to go abroad. Having lived in New Zealand all her life, she feels a strong urge to go off and explore the world.

Mobility is an issue for partners to consider. In terms of mobility, people who grew up abroad frequently have a different needs and attitudes than people who grew up in the home country. They may regularly feel the urge to move or

to return to an international lifestyle. Others may not want
to ever move again or, unlike other young people, do not
feel driven by the need to experience new things or see new
places — "I don't have to go places just so I can say I've seen
the world. I always feel like I'm new here anyway." Whatever the situation, they must discuss this issue with future
partners.

> Sandra grew up abroad. Within two years of marrying Jean
> Pierre and moving to France, she spoke fluent French and
> had been absorbed into Jean Pierre's circle of friends. Five
> years later, growing increasingly unhappy, she realized that
> while she had changed everything in her life, Jean Pierre
> had made few changes, and this had set the pattern for the
> rest of their relationship. Belatedly, she tried to find a more
> equal balance but failed. She moved back to Canada with
> their two young boys.

*Adaptability can be taken too far and become a handicap in rela-
tionships.* Because expatriate children become highly adaptable, they are often able and willing to make compromises in
relationships. They can accept differences and perceive other
people's needs. They strive to understand the other's view-
points—but don't always receive the same understanding in
return. Others are not as flexible or as accustomed to making compromises. As a result, they may find it difficult to
establish a balance in relationships.

Loneliness

All expatriate children have experienced intense loneliness. Loneliness is always painful, particularly for children. They are
more likely to believe that it is somehow their fault or that
there is something wrong with them. Adolescents suffer
acutely if they are excluded from social groups. Some children get so used to being lonely that they become loners and
give up trying to make friends. Because their experiences are
so different from those of others, they may believe that there
is no one they can relate to and that they are so unique that
no one could possibly understand them.

Unresolved Emotions

Expatriate children don't have much say in moving. We say go, they go—away from their familiar environment and far from friends, schools, and favorite things. This usually causes a variety of emotions: grief, anger, frustration, helplessness. Children need acknowledgement and acceptance of these reactions and need help in finding ways to express them. As parents, we often are not good at either accepting our children's emotions or allowing them to express them. Sadness makes us feel guilty; anger sparks irritation. "Don't we have enough to deal with already?" Some children, seeing how difficult moving is, want to spare us extra worry and do not share their grief or anger with us. In all these cases children sublimate their emotions, hiding them even from themselves—but these feelings do not go away.

Children carry unresolved emotions into adulthood. Grief, anger, or feelings of helplessness that were not expressed at the time may affect children's lives long after they have grown to adulthood. Unresolved grief can cause depression even decades later. Unexpressed anger can sour our relationships with our children. Children themselves may find their emotions hard to accept. As adults, for instance, they recognize parents' motives and difficulties, but the anger remains. Eventually these emotions must be discussed and resolved, however painful this may be. In some cases children should seek professional help in unraveling the unresolved issues that continue to affect their lives.

Chapter 16
Going Home

Twelve-year-old Jenny was going home. She had spent vacations at home in Australia since she was 4 years old and was looking forward to returning. But at her new school in a small town she had no idea what the other girls were talking about. She didn't know anything about horses, and they were not interested in Rome or London or the things she knew about. However, within a few weeks her accent matched theirs and she had caught up with the local TV series. Her parents felt that she was adjusting well, but one day she came home in tears. "I just don't feel like myself anymore. The others don't understand me. They're not even interested."

The hardest move is going home. When going abroad we anticipate problems and prepare for them. Going back to our own country should be easy. Unfortunately, it is not. Time marches on, and our familiar world has changed. The corner store has disappeared and our running group disbanded. Even more unnerving, we have changed. We have new interests, and we miss warm weather, the opera, or papaya for break-fast. We see everything through new eyes. "Our" city may now seem shabby and dirty. The longer the absence, the harder it is to readjust.

For children, the differences are even more dramatic. Things have changed more for them. Their friends have new friends. The things children do and talk about change rapidly, and chil-dren cannot rely on what they knew before. Their memories of home are vague and less vivid than the new customs they have learned and the experiences they have had in host coun-tries and in schools abroad.

> I fit in okay, but some things are weird. In the changing rooms in Rome everybody just got undressed. It was no big deal. Here all the girls hide themselves. They thought I was an exhibitionist, so now I get dressed under a big towel.

Children grow up. When they go home they are no longer at the same developmental stage—no longer in kindergarten but in high school, for instance. Their peers now have dif-ferent interests. There are new demands on them. How are you supposed to behave in high school? What does every-one talk about?

When returning home, culture shock is as much a reality as it is when going abroad. This is now widely recognized, and the reaction is referred to as "reverse culture shock." Expect your children to go through an adjustment process similar to that which they went through when moving abroad. As with cul-ture shock, they are likely to be excited about being home but then start finding fault, encountering difficulties, or feel-ing miserable. It usually takes several months for them to settle down and feel at home.

Preparing to Go Home

Getting ready to go home is as important as preparing to go abroad. Helping children get ready for the transition back home is a balancing act between encouraging them to get interested in things at home and allowing them to take time to say goodbye.

They should enjoy their final time abroad with their friends. It should be a time for consolidating these friendships, which will be valuable links to their international lives. Staying in contact with friends helps children retain an important part of their past as well as an international network for the future.

Involve your children in your preparations. Encourage them to reconnect with friends at home, find out about their new schools, and catch up on the latest news and gossip. The Internet is a wonderful tool. Even if your children haven't seen the latest TV series, they can look up what is happening. Ask friends and relatives to send recent children's magazines. Think of some interesting things to do when you arrive home to give your children something to look forward to. Allow some time for exploring when you get home, especially if your destination is new to children. Many people take a trip before coming home to allow some transition time. Others prefer to get back home and start moving on as soon as possible.

To prepare for a return home:
- *Catch up on home issues.* Help your children catch up on local news, music, sports, fashion, and TV series.
- *Renew contact with friends and relatives* so your children can reconnect with home before leaving the host country.
- *Don't disconnect too early.* Encourage your children to make the most of their remaining time with their friends and the host country.
- *Plan some interesting things to do upon returning home* to give your children something to look forward to. Treat going home as another adventure. Buy a guidebook and discover your country all over again.

From Global to Local

Going home means leaving the global village. In many ways expatriates live in a big, scattered community. People who live abroad for a long time find that every time they move they meet people they have known elsewhere or friends of friends. When we go home we leave this network behind. We also leave behind many of the privileges associated with being an expatriate. For children, these include private schools, being able to travel, and possibly having more pocket money.

Expatriate children get used to being special. It's not always comfortable being a foreigner, but at least you don't get lost in the crowd. Appearance, language, and behavior set you apart. Even when children go home on vacation, friends and relatives are glad to see them and make a fuss over them. International schools are often small, and children in those schools get personal attention. But when they go home they may attend large schools with more students per class. Suddenly they are just one of the crowd.

As foreigners, people expect us to be different. When we make a mistake we are excused, to some extent. When we go home we are expected to be the same as everyone else. We should just fit right back in and know how everything works. But often we don't remember, or things have changed. Children remember even less, and they're also older now. There is a new set of expectations, a new list of things they should know or should be able to do. They should know all the subtle, but often unspoken, rules about dating at home, for example, or be able to drive a car.

> Karla went home to attend college after spending most of her life abroad. She says, "There weren't many foreigners at the university and I wasn't one either. I was even more peculiar, an 'Aussie' but not an 'Aussie.' People that I'd never met seemed to know about me and about my life. It was strange."

Sometimes expatriate children are too different for comfort. Having lived in Mali, Jordan, and Iran can make them outsiders. Other children do not understand their experiences and may find them threatening. To fit in, expatriate children often stop talking about their experiences. As a result, many come to feel that they understand their friends but that their friends don't understand them.

Some expatriate children end up with others who are also different in some way. In many cases this is a positive thing. These children may be foreigners or may have become outsiders because of social ineptitude or a disability, but some are outcasts because of serious social or psychological problems. If this is the case, encourage your children to join a variety of activity groups so that healthier alternatives are available to them. Other expatriate children will also understand many of their experiences, so help your children maintain contact with friends overseas or other expatriate children.

> Florin and Noah have been living on different sides of the world for seven years, ever since both were evacuated from Liberia. Five times they have been able to meet during the summer, but they find writing difficult and rarely communicate during the rest of the year.

Children often find it difficult to keep up long-distance friendships. Their relationship skills are not well developed. They may be too young to write or may not like writing. However, e-mailed photos, chat lines, and an occasional telephone call can help keep friends close. Even when children lose interest in old friends because they are now so involved at home, parents should keep up with their friends' families. Children's long-distance communication is often sporadic, and sometimes they need an address so that they can catch up with friends even years later.

Support your children's international interests. Children often feel that they have lost a piece of themselves because they find it difficult to use the skills and knowledge they learned while abroad. Encourage them to take every opportunity to use this special knowledge—by doing school projects on countries they lived in, or on rainforests or volcanoes, for instance. Help them find appropriate outlets for their skills. Bragging about things they can do does not help them fit in. Using their knowledge in a group project does. Look for clubs where they can continue a sport or activity. Take vacations in countries where other languages are spoken, or get videos or magazines in those languages.

Encourage an international outlook. Children get absorbed in their personal worlds. This is natural and necessary, especially when they are adapting to their home country, but if they show interest in other places or events, take time to talk about it or get further information.

To help children remain international:

- *Help your children maintain contact with their friends around the world.* They often don't have the skills to keep up long-distance relationships. Help them send e-mails or photos, or let them call from time to time.
- *Encourage them to keep up special interests and skills.* Find interest and activity groups. Encourage them to use special knowledge and skills.
- *Foster an international perspective.* When they show interest in an international topic, be willing to discuss it with them or look for further information.

Fitting In at Home

In expatriate communities new children are welcomed. Everybody was a newcomer at one time or another and knows what it is like. International schools are set up to help new students settle down as soon as possible. At home, people are not oriented toward newcomers in the same way and often can't relate to their difficulties. However, they often are still willing to help. Enlist the help of teachers if your children are having difficulties at school. There may be other children who are willing to "show them the ropes." Ask friends and relatives to include your children in activities.

Expatriate children will experience a variety of reactions from their peers. Some will be interested in what they have been doing; many will not. Prague may as well be on the moon, for all they care. It's just not something they can relate to. Expatriate children may also encounter jealousy, or children who are threatened by those who have done things they haven't. Talk to your children about these different reactions. Encourage them to persist in looking for friends who share their interests and accept their experiences.

> Fifteen-year-old Melissa says, "I read about going home and I knew that the other kids would probably not really be interested in what I had been doing, so I let them tell me what they had been doing. It helped me catch up on things, but I felt kind of lonely because no one wanted to know about me. After a few weeks, though, one or two kids started asking me about living in Gabon."

Expatriate children who have gone through reentry recommend keeping a low profile, listening at least as much as talking, and showing an interest in what has been happening at home. Other children are more likely to take an interest in expatriate children's experiences if they know that their knowledge is also valued.

Part of reverse culture shock is being negative about home. Just as most of us go through a phase of being particularly negative about our host country, this reaction is also common when we go home. Not surprisingly, people tend to be sensitive about this attitude: "Well, why don't you go back to ——, then?" Help your children understand that seeing faults in your own country is normal after being away but that their friends probably won't appreciate hearing about all the things that are wrong with their country or city or school. Encourage them to express their frustration at home. At the same time, help them appreciate the good things and find things they like.

To help children fit in at home:

- *Show understanding of difficulties.* Help your children accept the fact that it takes time to learn how things work in the home country.
- *Build a support network.* Encourage your children to find someone who can "show them the ropes." Discuss integration problems with teachers. Enlist the help of friends and relatives.
- *Help your children develop integration skills* such as

showing an interest in others and keeping a low profile
initially.

* *Encourage your children to avoid negativity.* Accept
negative feelings about the home country, but encourage your children to express them at home rather than
at school. Help them find things they like.

Going Home Alone

George was excited about going home for college. After four
years in Bahrain he could finally start living his own life, but
the challenges he met were not the ones he expected. He didn't
know manage a bank account or balance a checkbook. Everyone could drive except him. He was overwhelmed by trying to organize his life as well as juggle his classes, and he
dropped two courses in the second semester.

*Expatriate children going home for college are unfamiliar with
things that their peers take for granted,* whether it is operating a
bank account or knowing what to talk about at parties. Many
are quite mature for their age in many ways, having flown
around the world alone or spent vacations far from their family. Adapting to a new environment is something they've had
a lot of practice at, but they may still struggle with this move.
They are now "at home" and expected to know how things
work there. They have to organize things that their parents
have taken responsibility for in other moves. And often their
family is very far away. However, preparation and support
can keep stress levels down and help students make a success of their college years.

Long-Term Preparations

Being able to manage practical skills makes the transition easier.
Unfortunately, expatriate children do not become autonomous
in the same way as peers at home. Although they can fly around
the world, they often cannot drive or were not allowed to work
in host countries, for instance. Start preparing your children

early. Give them opportunities to learn how to manage their own affairs, from washing clothes to managing their money. It is better for children to learn to do things—and make the inevitable mistakes—while they are still at home and we can help them if something goes wrong.

Let your children use as many services as possible, both abroad and at home. Encourage them to go to the post office or go shopping, to use public phones, to rent videos or use a laundromat. Children also need experience in dealing with authorities. Let them buy their monthly bus passes or go through passport checks on their own as soon as they are old enough.

Children should learn how to manage money. The principles of budgeting are the same with small or large amounts, but it is better for children to make mistakes with pocket money than with tuition fees. Open a bank account at home that your children can use while on vacation, or create a family banking system in which they can earn interest on pocket money. If your children are going to have a credit card while in college, give it to them some time before they leave home. Start with a low limit.

Choosing a College or University

Studying in a home country has advantages. It is usually cheaper than in other countries, although many require previous residency in the country or state to qualify for lower fees. European Union countries usually require two years of residency somewhere in the Union. Young people also develop a strong relationship to the country where they spend their college years. It is an ideal time for those who have grown up abroad to get to know their country, especially if they have been abroad a long time. As most will eventually work in their own country, they can also make contacts that will be useful in the job market.

If possible, choose a college with an international student body. Children who have lived abroad often feel more comfortable in a multicultural environment. The e-mails and letters of expatriate students are frequently laced with "My friend from Benin...." or "My Cuban mate...."

Organize accommodations early. There are often waiting lists for good student accommodations. Student housing is ideal for students from abroad when they first arrive, especially if there is a cafeteria. They have enough to get used to without having to worry about paying rent and utilities or cooking. If your children are in student housing, find out if they can stay there during vacations or long weekends.

Easing the Transition

If possible, accompany your children to college. They're usually quite capable of getting there and settling in themselves, but it is a lonely and stressful process. If you go with them, you can identify potential problems. You will also be able to picture where they are when you are back abroad. Don't take over any tasks that they would rather do themselves. Although most students have enough to tackle when settling in and are glad to have some help, respect their independence.

Money is a major theme for all students. Ask colleges for information about student budgets to give you an idea of how much money your children will need and to give them an idea of how much they should be spending on various items. Colleges sometimes are not oriented toward people coming from abroad. Payment methods may be tailored to people living in the country, so you may have to work out alternative methods of payment.

Necessary infrastructure:
- *Money flows.* Set up bank accounts and means of transfer and withdrawal. Find out how various fees can be paid.
- *Communication systems.* How will your children call home? How will you reach them? Make sure they have access to a computer and e-mail.

- *Health care services.* Children living alone usually need separate or different health insurance from yours. Locate a family doctor or student health service as well as a dentist. Find out how these can be paid.

Contact friends and relatives, especially those who live close by, and ask them to call your children or invite them to dinner every now and then. Your children may not take them up on the invitations, but it's good to know that there's someone out there.

Preparing students to go home alone:

- *Prepare students.* Help them learn the skills they will need when going home alone: taking care of personal needs, managing money, using various services, dealing with authorities.
- *Choose a college with an international student body, if possible.* Expatriate children often feel more at home in an international environment.
- *Organize accommodation early.* There are often waiting lists for good student accommodation.
- *Accompany your children to college, if possible.* Most children can do it alone if necessary, but it is very stressful.
- *Make sure the necessary infrastructure is in place* — a banking system, communication facilities, health insurance.

Issues

Driving

Senta learned to drive when she got to New Zealand, but for the first eighteen months she only had a provisional license and couldn't drive after 10 o'clock at night. Although this makes sense for the 16-year-olds who have just gotten their license, it created a problem for a 20-year-old girl living on her own.

In many countries children cannot drive until they are 18 years old. As a result, many expatriate children go home to college unable to drive. This is a problem in countries where most people are dependent on cars and there is not much public transportation. In some cases it is possible to get a license during vacations, but you often have to be a resident to take the test. Learner drivers also are not usually allowed to use rental cars. If your children turn 18 before they leave for college, make learning to drive a priority if they will need to drive at home. In some countries, although children cannot get a license until they are 18, they can start learning beforehand.

Vacations

Your home is still their home. In the first year or so away from home, your children will usually think of your house as home. As long as they don't have their own home, keep a place for them in yours. If possible, keep their room intact, or at least keep a closet or two reserved for them. Do not throw away their things, even if you think they are useless. Let them sort them out when they come home.

Home is far away. Even when your children come home at regular intervals, there will be short vacations or long weekends when other students can go home but your children can't. Discuss other options with them: exploring the home country, staying with friends or relatives, catching up on work. Call them during this time. Send e-mails and a small package.

> Rosie says, "The first time Elias came home was terrible. He argued with his father all the time. He even threatened to leave at one point. I know he was just establishing his independence and his right to make his own decisions, but he used sledgehammer methods to do it. The next time he came home, I was almost dreading it, but it was okay. Maybe he thought we'd got the message by then."

When your children come home, they are not the same as when they went away. They are used to making their own decisions and may resent having to fit into the family again.

Discuss issues such as going out at night. You can no longer set rules, but you can ask them to show respect—to let you know if they are going to be late, for instance. Take time to catch up again, to listen to what they have been doing and their new ideas.

> I was just devastated the first time our daughter said she wouldn't be home for Christmas. I just felt that it wouldn't really be Christmas at all. In the end we got together with some friends and it was different, but okay.

Respect your children's wishes. Avoid getting angry when they don't come home. Often they would like to be home, but something else is just more important this time. Send e-mails and packages and keep in touch. Children sometimes do not come home because they cannot work in the host country or don't have any friends there. Even if they have lived there at some time, their friends may be in college, and after a week or two they get bored and lonely. If your children are coming home, plan some interesting things to do, such as going to plays or concerts or visiting new places.

The Empty Nest

> When Sophie left Larnaca to go to college in England, her mother said, "Life got so quiet. It was as if half the town had moved away. The telephone stopped ringing non-stop and I missed all Sophie's friends dropping by. After years of helping out at the school, I don't have anything to do there either."

The time when the last child leaves home is a tough time for expatriates. Their children are far away. International schools, a primary social center of expatriate life, cease to be a source of social interaction. To avoid isolation, at-home spouses should join groups outside the school before their children leave. For some spouses, traveling with employees when they go on business trips is an option.

Shrink distances as much as possible. Use the Internet and telephone to keep in touch. Snail mail will also be welcome, so send postcards and small parcels. Put aside a few moments each day just to think about your children—to wish them well, say a prayer, or light a candle. Find out the fastest way to get to your children in case of an emergency.

Chapter 17
Crises Abroad

In May 2000 Joe was diagnosed with a brain tumor. An employee of a multinational company, Joe lived in Cairo with his wife Angelina and their three boys. Within two days he was on a plane home with his family for an operation to remove the tumor. Three weeks later Angelina returned to pack up the house. She says, "The tumor was not malignant, thank goodness, but Joe picked up an infection and was ill for a long time. We lived with my parents until our stuff arrived from Cairo, which was a strain for all of us. The boys fought all the time. They missed their friends at school and hated the cold weather. We didn't know if Joe would be able to keep his job. It was a terrible time, but we were lucky to have friends and family to help us out."

Crises abroad are particularly traumatic. Even at home people become ill, have accidents, or suffer nervous breakdowns. Companies go bankrupt or lose contracts. But if you are living overseas the impact is greater. For one thing, we cannot deal with crises as competently abroad as at home. Most expatriates don't know their way around in foreign places as well as they do in their own city or country. Our support network is often inadequate, especially if we have not been in a place very long. When we have to return home, we often have nowhere to go. As a result, the impact of crises is worse. They are more likely to be traumatic for us and for our children.

When something happens abroad, expatriates often have to leave: to get treatment for a seriously ill family member, to find another job when a company goes bankrupt or when a country dissolves into political unrest. In many cases we leave in a hurry or under less than ideal circumstances. We cannot pack up in an orderly fashion, or others have to do the packing for us. In political crises we may simply pack a suitcase and leave everything else behind. In most cases there is not much chance to say goodbye. Home, schools, and daily routines are left behind, as are employees, friends, and sometimes pets. Moreover, when we have to leave in a hurry, things are not ready for us at home. We have not organized accommodation . Even if we still have a house in our home country, it is often rented out. In some cases leaving means the loss of a job.

Dealing with Crises

Departures due to crises are stressful and disorienting. Illness of a family member, the collapse of business, or a political crisis are nerve-racking enough without the problems of leaving a foreign country and returning home. The nature of such exits causes another set of problems. When we leave in a hurry, the whole fabric of our lives disintegrates from one moment to the next—daily routines, familiar environment, friends, work, schools. This sudden loss of structure leaves most people in a state of disorientation and mental confusion. Returning to an unsure future and temporary living conditions extends the state of limbo, and for many people it can be a long time before they are able to reorient themselves.

Crises are frightening for children. They often don't understand
what is going on. They know that their parents are upset or
even scared. The pattern of their lives may change overnight.
Suddenly they are on a plane home, without understanding
why. Children also have fewer tools to help put their lives together again. They can't find themselves a school or organize
a household. Keeping some semblance of order and normality
through a crisis is a challenge for parents, but it is very important for children. It is also a healthy focus for us.

Always keep your children informed. Explain a situation as simply as possible. They are most interested in what a situation means for *them:* whether they will have to leave their
friends, or where they will go to school when you get home.
If you don't know anything, tell them you will let them know
as soon as you find out. If your children are worried or frightened, offer comfort.

*If you have to leave your children with others for some reason,
explain carefully* how long they will be staying and what arrangements have been made in terms of school or activities. Promise to call them at specific times, and stick to that
schedule. If these arrangements change, let your children
know as soon as possible.

If you are not leaving immediately, carry on as usual. No matter
where you are—in your home, at a hotel, or staying with
friends—stick to normal routines as much as possible. Cook
familiar foods. Do things that your children find comforting and fun.

Leaving

If you have to leave, take time for goodbyes, if possible. Even if
time is of the essence, encourage your children to call their
friends. If you can't say goodbye before you leave, allow your
children to call their friends after they arrive home. Get contact addresses. Children should say goodbye to household
personnel. If you have to leave without pets, discuss it with
your children. Tell them what arrangements you have made
to ensure that the pets are cared for.

If you leave home in a hurry, you may have to leave possessions behind. Most of the things we own we don't absolutely need, but if we lose them all at once, connections to our daily lives and our past are lost. It is therefore tempting to go abroad with only the most necessary items, but children need familiar things when they live in a foreign country. However, be realistic. Keep negatives and copies of photos out of the country or e-mail photos home, if possible. Store a few items from all phases of your children's lives elsewhere. Take only copies of essential papers. If you really need the originals, keep copies elsewhere.

When leaving, let your children choose what they want to take with them. If you leave under uncertain circumstances, you may or may not be able to take the rest of your possessions, or it may take a long time. Explain this to your children and let them choose their favorite things. Pack things that cannot be replaced. Family videos may be more important than jewelry, for instance.

Arriving Home

Arriving home is a great relief. It is also the moment when the adrenaline stops running and we are confronted with all sorts of existential problems. Where can we live? Should we put our children in school? Often there is little support because other people believe that everything is okay now that we are home. The problem is that very little is okay. The future is unsure, our children are upset, and we are disoriented.

> Margrit organized trick-or-treat for Senta and Sascha in her neighborhood in Switzerland—definitely a first in the village. Her friends handed out candy to the children when they knocked on their doors. Many Halloweens have come and gone, but this is the one our children remember. It was also the turning point in recovering from the sudden loss of their home.

Support is an important factor in surviving. The one good thing about crises is the support you receive from others, sometimes from unexpected quarters. However, many people don't understand that your problems are not over when you arrive home, so if you need something, ask. Sometimes friends simply don't know what to do, but they may be happy to help if you let them know what you need. Children also need support. Peers can be cruel with children who are feeling insecure, and traumatized children are sometimes aggressive or, alternatively, subdued and uncommunicative. Talk to teachers and ask them to watch for difficulties. Sometimes children want to talk about their experiences at school, but they should not be forced to talk if they don't feel like it.

Effects of Crises on Children

Two months after leaving Zaire, Evan's parents still avoided raising their voices to their 6-year-old, who interpreted everything as a threat. Simple rebukes by his teacher robbed him of sleep. Anyone in uniform, even the conductor on a train, provoked a frightened and angry reaction.

Children exhibit a variety of reactions to crisis situations, depending on their temperament and experiences. Almost all children show some signs of distress, often in the form of an increase in misbehavior or bad moods. Commonly, young children regress temporarily, becoming more dependent, starting to wet the bed again, or behaving immaturely for their age. Some suffer from nightmares. Teenagers are more likely to respond with depression or moodiness.

Typical reactions to crises or traumatic events:

- *Preschool children:* aggression, changes in eating and sleeping habits, separation anxiety, loss of recently acquired developmental skills such as toilet training or language skills.
- *School-age children:* the same problems as above, but also anger, social problems, school phobia, difficulty concentrating, depression.
- *Adolescents:* depression and sadness, anxiety, self-deprecation, apathy, acting out, difficulty concentrating, diminished interest in activities, decreased confidence in the future.

Strong emotional reactions to crises are normal. However, some reactions are beyond parents' ability to cope with, and children will need professional help. Experiences that overwhelm children's ability to cope or change their frame of reference can cause trauma, and some children who have been through a crisis will suffer from post-traumatic stress disorder (PSTD). Symptoms include flashbacks, nightmares, phobias, or not being able to think about anything else. Children may be severely disoriented, be overwhelmed by anger, or become antisocial. If your children display these symptoms, seek help as soon as possible. The most effective treatment for trauma is the most immediate.

> Five years after leaving Afghanistan, and quite independently, Nancy's children both began writing about the coup they had experienced. As a result, they discussed memories, some for the first time, of how Nancy had turned up the music to drown out the helicopter gunships shelling the king's palace. "When I hear those songs, I still think of Kabul and gunfire," her son said.

The effects of crises reemerge from time to time. Children must often work through their experiences at each stage of development — to grasp what happened with the comprehension of a 6-year-old, a 12-year-old, an 18-year-old. Be prepared to discuss events, even if they happened years before. Encourage children's efforts to integrate past happenings through writing, doing school projects, or talking. Behavioral problems may recur at these different stages. Major events or changes in children's lives, such as moving, may trigger these. When such events occur, keep an eye on your children. If necessary, seek professional help.

Some children take on adult roles. Seeing that their parents are stressed or can't cope with the demands of the moment, some children take on parenting roles with their siblings or even with their parents. Sometimes this can't be helped, but make sure that these children also receive comfort and that they are encouraged to return to their appropriate roles as soon as possible.

To help children deal with crises:

- *Keep your children informed.* Tell them what is happening, simply and without frightening details. Explain how the crisis will affect them. If something changes, let them know as soon as possible.
- *Say goodbyes, if possible.* Let your children call or visit their friends if time allows. If not, let them call when you arrive home.
- *Let your children choose what they want to take with them.*
- *Build a support network at home.* Help your children find appropriate support. Let teachers know that your children may need extra support. Accept all help that is offered.
- *Be understanding of behavioral reactions to the situation.* However, set limits. Help your children express emotions in an appropriate way. If your children are severely disturbed, seek professional help as soon as possible.

Healing and Moving On

Crises are also an opportunity for new beginnings and for growth. Children who master difficult situations gain confidence that they can handle such events in the future. They learn that life goes on even in the face of difficulties. However, to grow stronger rather than being defeated by events, children need comfort and guidance. It is a real challenge to help children when we are dealing with all the other problems caused by a crisis, but many of the things we can do for our children also help us.

> Twelve years after a hasty exit from a country in Africa, Sylvia said to her mother, "You know, I've read about trauma and I wondered why I didn't really suffer from the things that happened to us. I think it didn't affect me because you and Dad made us feel safe."

Children's sense of security is very subjective. This is a great asset for parents. Even in difficult times we can help them feel more secure. We can diminish the psychological impact of crises and help them work through the aftermath. It is almost impossible to stay calm all the time, but we can put as much normality, comfort, security, and fun into our children's lives as possible.

As far as possible, stick to familiar routines and rules. This provides security and helps everyone reorient. Be understanding. If your children resist going to bed or are afraid of being alone, for instance, maintain their bedtime but allow them to sleep in your room or with the light on. Make a home, no matter how temporary. Put up a few posters; hang your children's paintings on the refrigerator; buy some flowers.

> In the dark, cold days before Christmas, Danielle's children had to catch an early train to school. Coming from a sunny home in the Middle East, which they had had to leave because of a canceled business contract, they were miserable. To help them face the day, Danielle put small advent gifts in their bags every day, to be opened on the way to school.

Positives balance negatives. Favorite things, fun events, interesting outings, and so forth help raise children's spirits. Even small things are effective: a treat when children arrive home from school, a favorite meal, time to play a game or do a puzzle. Celebrate everything that you can think of: birthdays, anniversaries, e-mails from old friends, making a new friend. Let your children know that it is okay to smile and to have fun. In crisis situations children lose confidence in the future. Losing a home overnight, for example, decreases their confidence in the world. Help them reanchor themselves by giving them things to look forward to. Plan outings—a trip to the zoo or a movie. Talk about future plans such as vacations.

> Briska says, "Every picture André drew had black ghosts in it. After about three weeks the ghosts got smaller. Eventually they were just little figures in the corner, and he started using more colors, too."

Children need opportunities to express their feelings about what has happened, but don't force it. Let them choose the time. When they want to talk, make time to listen. Have drawing materials, clay, building blocks, and the like available so your children can express themselves in other ways. Many will work through their emotions by these means.

Show understanding for disruptive behaviors, but set limits. Some of the effects of a crisis, such as bed wetting, should be accepted without comment. In other cases children must find more appropriate outlets for their frustration and anger. Show understanding for these emotions, but stop destructive behavior. Suggest alternative ways to vent aggression. "I know you are angry, but you can't hit your sister. Would you like us to go outside to the playground, or would you like to draw a picture?" Find opportunities for exercise.

Grief is normal after a loss. Children who leave a place suddenly lose many of the things they were attached to. As far as young children are concerned, the things they left behind are gone. Talk about being sad and about leaving behind people or pets. Give your children opportunities to cry or express anger about their losses.

Children are often ready to move on sooner than adults. Just as they grieve more readily, they are often ready to make news friends sooner or get involved in activities sooner than we are. Encourage them to make the most of their opportunities and to find things they like. Take advantage of being at home. Spend time with relatives and friends. Help your children catch up on things in the home country through outings, TV, magazines, and visits with friends.

To help children recover from crises and move on:
- *Provide as much security as possible.* Pay special attention to what makes your children *feel* secure.
- *Create as normal and calm an environment as possible.* Stick to normal routines. Keep your usual guidelines and rules, but be understanding.
- *Balance negatives with positives.* Do things that your children enjoy. Let them know that it is okay to smile and have fun.
- *Encourage your children to express their grief.* This is

normal under the circumstances, but help them find appropriate outlets.
- *Allow your children to move on.* Children may be ready to move on faster than we are. Encourage their involvement in new activities and interests.
- *Take advantage of being home again.* Visit relatives. Catch up on local events.

Medical Emergencies

In 1990, as the result of injuries received in a fall from a horse, 15-year-old Jean went into renal failure. Doctors in Lubumbashi, Zaire, told his parents that they did not have the facilities to treat him and that without treatment he could not live more than eight to ten hours. His father immediately called an air rescue service in South Africa, and Jean arrived at a hospital in Johannesburg just in time.

Often our biggest enemy in foreign countries is lack of knowledge. We do not know what care is available or how to get it. In some countries there is limited medical care and evacuation is our most important medical asset. Even when medical care is adequate, many expatriates prefer to go home when a family member becomes very ill or is seriously injured. We feel more comfortable and competent at home and have more confidence in our own medical system. Take out insurance to cover medical evacuation with an ambulance jet or on a scheduled flight, as this is enormously expensive.

To prepare for medical emergencies:
- *Get information about emergency services.* If you cannot communicate in the local language, find someone whom you can reach at any time to help you. In many countries your family doctor can help you get fast and competent treatment.
- *Organize good medical insurance,* including coverage of medical evacuation. Find out which form of evacuation is fastest.

Business Crises

In 1999, while he was living in Tbilisi, Georgia, with his wife and two daughters, Vladimir's company declared bankruptcy. The company ceased to pay his salary, but because Vladimir could not pay company debts to local businesses and employees, he was unable to leave the country. The children's quarterly school fees remained unpaid, and the girls had to leave school. The family also had to leave their apartment because of unpaid rent. Fortunately, they were able to move in with friends. After two months Vladimir's wife and children were granted exit visas, but Vladimir had to remain another three months until the payment of company debts could be organized.

Expatriates are often dependent on their organizations to cover the high costs of living in other countries, private schools, and medical care. They also frequently rely on company financial facilities. They may not have a local bank account, for instance. The disappearance of this support can leave expatriates high and dry. A bankrupt company is not even able to pay repatriation costs. If your company is working on a contract basis in the host country, make sure *your* contract deals with the eventuality of cancelation of this contract. Also determine whether loss of possessions or the costs of an evacuation are covered in the event of political upheaval. Keep in touch with colleagues at the head office so that you will hear about rumors of financial difficulties or takeovers in your company. Secure your situation as much as possible. Pay school fees for the year so that your children's education is ensured as long as you are in the country. Do the same with rent if this is paid by the company, and with insurance premiums.

Legally, expatriates are often at a disadvantage. In many countries, if there are legal battles to be fought, foreigners are at a disadvantage because they do not know their rights, because of xenophobic attitudes, or because of a corrupt system that they cannot manipulate as well as locals can. In countries in which you need an exit visa, you can be more or less held hostage if something goes wrong. In other cases, national or international regulations do not work in your favor. We can only collect unemployment benefits in the host country, for instance, and they may be a lot lower than those paid in the home country. Or, if your right of residence is linked to your employment status, your host country may demand that you leave immediately and thus effectively avoid paying unemployment benefits. Forewarned is forearmed. Get information about national and international laws and agreements. Check the extent of your personal liability in case your company encounters financial difficulties. If necessary, take out private insurance to cover shortfalls in earnings or legal costs.

To prepare for business emergencies:
- *Check your work contract carefully* to see what is contracted in case of the cancelation of a contract or a political emergency.
- *Check host-country laws and international agreements.* What is the extent of your personal liability in case of problems? If you become unemployed, can you collect unemployment benefits in your home country or only in your host country?
- *Follow company events carefully.* Maintain contact with colleagues at home so that you will be forewarned of possible difficulties.
- *Secure your position.* Pay school fees for the whole year and health insurance and rent as far ahead as possible.
- *Keep some liquid assets* in case of emergency.

Political Crises

Images of expatriates hastily exiting a country because of political unrest regularly flash around the world. Political upheavals in a host country are frightening, especially if you have children with you. Consider the political situation of a country before accepting a posting. It is quite reasonable to refuse a posting to a politically unstable country when you have children. If

you do accept, develop concrete strategies for dealing with
potential crises.

> The school bus was already 15 minutes late, and Alisée and
> her 7-year-old son were getting impatient. Alisée was just
> wondering at the stillness of the street when a burst of gun-
> fire sounded close by. She hastily pulled her son back in-
> side the gate and ran into the house with him. This was
> their first indication of trouble, although others had known
> about the coup hours before.

Plan for emergencies. Register at your embassy. Invest in good
communication equipment to keep in touch with family
members, friends, and embassies. Keep lists of emergency
numbers and contacts handy and develop a network of people
to warn each other of trouble—but avoid rumormongers.
Keep supplies of food in the house. When you buy a car, consider evacuation. If you are likely to leave by car over bad
roads, invest in a four-wheel drive vehicle.

> Before making a hasty exit from Brazzaville, Melanie packed
> essential items for her family. When they arrived at a hotel
> in Libreville, she unpacked her bag and found a box of
> condoms that had been gathering dust since her husband's
> vasectomy two years before! "I thought I was being very
> cool and collected. I guess I wasn't as focused as I thought
> I was," she says.

Crises don't promote clear thinking. Before trouble arises, make
a list of what to take and what to do before you leave. Prepare luggage. In orderly evacuations on commercial planes,
you can take the airline allowance, but don't turn up with
excess luggage. In other situations, the allowance is usually
just one small bag each. Take cash in case you need to pay
for anything on the way. Tell children how much luggage
they can take and let them choose what is important to
them. Work out exit routes—how to get to the embassy, airport, or port, bypassing important buildings or potential
roadblocks. Both parents should practice driving these
routes, as one parent may not be home when a crisis begins.

Ask the school what arrangements have been made in case of an emergency.

Discuss the situation with your children. There are likely to be a lot of rumors, and children will also hear them. Explain the situation as simply as possible, but avoid frightening details. Answer your children's questions honestly, but do not give them more information than they ask for. Deal with their fears sympathetically and provide as much comfort as possible.

In the meantime, carry on as usual. Everything may still turn out just fine, and normal routines and activities help everyone feel more secure. In stressful times, nutrition is doubly important. You need the energy, and it is not a good time to become ill, so cook the healthiest meals possible and hand around the vitamins. Try to lighten things up. Fun activities and laughter are good antidotes for fear and tension. Bake a cake or prepare your children's favorite meals. Consider what makes your children feel secure. Is it a bedtime story, a family meal, a game, sitting and talking? Make time for an extra hug or chat.

> Dan was a big man, a tower of strength, you would think—until trouble swept Chad up in a fury of street battles and looting. During a daytime lull in the fighting, a convoy was hastily organized to evacuate foreigners from around the city. No one knew how long the streets would maintain their eerie calm. Everyone hurried as much as possible—until they reached Dan's house, where the column ground to a halt. Tension mounted as sporadic gunfire rang out again, but Dan continued to shove and squeeze items into his car, determined to save every possible material item, seemingly oblivious to the safety of his family and others.

Everybody reacts differently to crises, and it is hard to tell how you will be affected. Focus on your children's needs as an incentive to stay calm. If there is shooting, move to the safest place in your house. Read stories or play games with your children. Simple games are best because everyone's concentration will be limited. Provide high-protein, high-energy food and plenty to drink. Avoid sugary foods or caffeine.

When it is time to leave the house, prepare the children. If you have news, talk to them about what has been happening and what they might see—a strong military presence, for instance. Keep it simple and avoid scary details. Give instructions as to how they should behave. Take along food and drink. Normal services are often disrupted, and there are bound to be delays. When you leave, take normal precautions, such as making sure your children wear seatbelts. Distract young children with a toy or book, if possible. Continue normal routines when possible. An airport terminal or the back of a truck can be the place for a nap, a story, a snack, a cuddle, or in the case of older children, a game of cards. Whenever possible, let children move around to release nervous energy.

To cope with political crises:

- *Keep emergency supplies* of food, water, and gas, or diesel if you run a generator.
- *Keep medical supplies.* Pharmacies are among the first places to be looted, so keep essentials on hand.
- *Make a list* of what you have to do and what to take with you in the event of a crisis.
- *Talk to your children about the situation,* simply and without frightening details.
- *CARRY ON AS USUAL.*

Appendixes

Appendix A: Situation of Employees of Various Types of Organizations

	Teachers	Army Personnel	Diplomats	Organizations (UN, World Bank)	Missionaries	Business Firms
Location	Usually in larger cities	May be isolated on army bases	Usually in capital city or large cities	Often in large cities	Sometimes in remote locations	Usually in large cities
Financial Situation	Moderate to good Contract basis	Moderate Secure	Good to very good Secure	Good to very good Often on contract basis	Poor to moderate Often little security	Good to excellent Limited security
Housing	Fair to very good	Reasonable	Very good to excellent	Good to excellent	Sometimes local rather than home standards	Good to excellent

	Teachers	Army Personnel	Diplomats	Organizations (UN, World Bank)	Missionaries	Business Firms
Support	Support from school community	Well-developed but rigid support structure	Good formal and informal support network	Good formal support; informal support variable	Support from religious community	Variable—zero to excellent
Travel	Usually 1 trip/year	Usually 1 trip/year Also depends on availability of army transport	Variable—many 1 trip/year; some 1 trip/2 years	Usually 1 trip/year Various allowances for nonresident children	Sometimes only 1 trip/ 3-5 years	Usually 1 trip/year Possibly rest-and-recreation trips
Emergency Situations	Limited protection	Well protected	Many have diplomatic immunity Protection varies with size of mission	Some personnel have diplomatic immunity Reasonable protection	Very exposed Limited funds	Limited protection

Appendix B: Cultural Parameters of Education

Schooling is part of children's acculturation. Each educational system reflects the culture from which it came, and international schools are no exception. The table below is not a comprehensive list of the cultural differences in education, nor does it necessarily apply to all international schools. It simply indicates some of the differences with which children and parents may be confronted.

Many International Schools	Other Educational Systems
Teaching materials and methods are expected to change and keep up with new knowledge and changing needs.	Teaching materials and methods are expected to stay the same.
Students and teachers are expected to express themselves in concise, clear language. Writer/speaker must make his or her meaning clear.	Students and teachers may use complex language. Reader or listener must find the meaning.
Students are rewarded for creativity in problem solving.	Students are rewarded for accuracy in problem solving.
Less structured learning situations, some self-determined objectives, broad assignments, and flexible timetables.	Structured learning situations, precise objectives, detailed assignments, and strict timetables.
Emphasis on self-discipline.	Emphasis on discipline.
Students should learn to learn. Emphasis on research and analytical skills.	Students should learn specified information. Emphasis on memorization skills.

Teachers and students have an informal relationship. Students are responsible for their own learning, depending on age. Students should identify their own problems and approach teachers.	Teacher and students have a formal relationship. Teachers are responsible for students' learning. Teachers should identify students' problems and approach students.
Student participation is encouraged.	Lessons take the form of lectures.
Students may ask questions of teachers and challenge what is taught.	Teachers ask questions of students. Students are not encouraged to challenge what is taught.
Participation of parents is expected.	Parents should leave teaching to the teachers.

Bibliography

Living Abroad

Black, J. Stewart, and Hal B. Gregerson, *So You're Going Overseas.* San Diego, CA: Global Business Publishers, 1999.

Kohls, Robert L., *Survival Kit for Overseas Living.* Yarmouth, ME: Intercultural Press, 1984.

Haour-Knipe, Mary, *Expatriation, Stress and Coping.* New York: Routledge, 2000.

Hughes, Katherine L., *The Accidental Diplomat: Dilemmas of the Trailing Spouse.* Putnam Valley, NY: Aletheia Publications, 1998.

Kalb, Rosalind, and Penelope Welch, *Moving your Family Overseas.* Yarmouth, ME: Intercultural Press, 1992.

Pascoe, Robin, *Surviving Overseas: A Wife's Guide to Successful Living.* Singapore: Times Books International, 1992.

———, *Culture Shock: Successful Living Abroad.* Portland, OR: Graphic Arts, 1993.

Piet-Pelon, Nancy, and Barbara Hornby, *Women's Guide to Overseas Living,* 2nd ed. Yarmouth ME: Intercultural Press, 1992.

Rabe, Monica, *Culture Shock! Successful Living Abroad: Living and Working Abroad.* Portland, OR: Graphic Arts Center Publishing, 1997.

Expatriate Children

Blohm, Judith M., *Where in the World Are You Going?* Yarmouth, ME: Intercultural Press, 1996.

> An activity book for children ages 5–10, to help them through the process of saying goodbye and traveling, and to prepare them for the move abroad.

Dyer, Jill, and Roger Dyer, *...and Bees Make Honey.* Kingswood, Australia: M. K. Merinma, 1995.

> An anthology of writings by expatriate children from all over the world.

Gordon, Alma, *Don't Pig Out on Junk Food: The MK's Guide to Survival in the U.S.* Wheaton, IL: EMIS, 1993.

> A practical but entertaining guide for MKs (missionary kids) on returning to the United States. Many issues mentioned also apply to other expatriate children.

McClusky, Karen Curnow, ed., *Notes from a Traveling Childhood.* Washington, DC: Foreign Service Youth Foundation, 1994.

> A collection of short essays written by adult third culture kids, as well as others working with expatriate children, about issues concerning international families.

Pascoe, Robin, *Living and Working Abroad: A Parent's Guide.* London: Kuperard, 1994.

> A very readable book dealing with the practical aspects of taking children abroad; covers topics ranging from giving birth overseas to how to handle home leave.

Pollock, David C., and Ruth E. Van Reken, *The Third Culture Kid Experience: Growing Up Among Worlds.* Yarmouth, ME: Intercultural Press, 1999.

> This very thorough book written by two of the best-known experts in this area looks at the experiences and issues of third culture kids, from who they are to their strengths and weaknesses.

Smith, Carolyn D., *The Absentee American: Repatriates' Perspectives on America.* Putnam Valley, NY: Aletheia Publications, 1994.

Describes overseas life, reentry into the United States, and the long-term effects of these experiences.

Taber, Sarah Mansfield, *Of Many Lands: Journal of a Traveling Childhood.* Washington, DC: Foreign Service Youth Foundation, 1997.

A journal designed for people raised in foreign countries, young or old. It combines short essays about the author's experiences with opportunities for readers to reflect on their own experiences.

Van Reken, Ruth E., *Letters Never Sent.* Elgin, IL: David C. Cook, 1988.

Written to her parents, these very moving letters tell of the experiences of an American woman who grew up in a missionary family in Africa.

Wertsch, Mary Edwards, *Military Brats: Legacies of Childhood Inside the Fortress.* Putnam Valley, NY: Aletheia Publications, 1991.

Analyzes the consequences—both positive and negative—of growing up in a military family.

Culture Shock and Transitions

Bridges, William, *Transitions: Making Sense of Life's Changes.* Reading, MA: Addison-Wesley, 1980.

———, *Managing Transitions: Making the Most of Change.* London: Nicholas Brealey, 1991.

Marx, Elisabeth, *Breaking Through Culture Shock: What You Need to Succeed in International Business.* London: Nicholas Brealey, 1999.

Moving

Nida, Patricia Cooney, and Wendy M. Heller, *The Teenager's Survival Guide to Moving.* New York: Macmillan, 1985.

Schubeck, Carol M., *Let's Move Together.* Orange, CA: Suitcase Press, 2000.

Shepard, Steven, *Managing Cross-Cultural Transition: A Handbook for Corporations, Employees, and Their Families.* Putnam Valley, NY: Aletheia Publications, 1998.

Reentry

Austin, Clyde N., ed., *Cross-cultural Re-entry: A Book of Readings.* Abilene, TX: Abilene Christian University, 1986.

Black, J. Stewart, and Hal B. Gregerson, *So You're Coming Home.* San Diego, CA: Global Business Publishers, 1999.

Smith, Carolyn D., ed., *Strangers at Home: Essays on the Effects of Living Overseas and Coming "Home" to a Strange Land.* Putnam Valley, NY: Aletheia Publications, 1996.

Storti, Craig, *The Art of Coming Home.* Yarmouth, ME: Intercultural Press, 1997.

International Education

Findlay, Bob, *International Education Handbook.* London: Kogan Page, 1997.

International Schools Services, *The ISS Directory of Overseas Schools, 2001/2002 Edition.* Princeton, NJ: International Schools Services.

Language Learning

Appel, René, and Pieter Muysken, *Language Contact and Bilingualism.* London: Edward Arnold, 1987.

Harding, Edith, and Philip Riley, *The Bilingual Family.* Cambridge: Cambridge University Press, 1987.

Marshall, Terry, *The Whole World Guide to Language Learning.* Yarmouth, ME: Intercultural Press, 1990.

General Parenting

Covey, Stephen R., and Sandra Merrill, *The 7 Habits of Highly Effective Families: Building a Beautiful Family Culture in a Turbulent World.* New York: Simon & Schuster, 1997.

Elias, Maurice J., Steven E. Tobias, and Brian S. Friedlander, *Raising EmotionallyIntelligent Teenagers: Parenting with Love, Laughter and Limits.* NY: Random House, 2000.

Fabe, Adel, and Elaine Mazlish, *How to Talk so Kids Will Listen and Listen so Kids Will Talk.* NY: Avon Books, 1980.

Seligman, Martin E. P., *The Optimistic Child.* NY: HarperCollins, 1996.

INDEX

international schools, 5, 6, 27, 96, 151, 152–154, 163, 165
     disadvantages of, 154
     and special-needs children, 94, 168
     types of, 152
International Schools Service, 160
international skills. *See* skills, cross-cultural
internationalism, 202–203, 214, 215
intolerance, 178–180

Job description, 23–24
Jordan, Kathleen Finn, 151n, 199n

Language, 4, 82, 97, 98. *See also* educational language
     courses, 165–166
     home, 142
     host-country, 140, 142–143, 146–147
     learning, 140–149, 166–167
     making choices about, 141–143
     mother tongue, maintaining, 147–149, 167
     teachers, 146
Lateral Thinking for Management (De Bono), 203n
legal issues, 121–122, 234–235
Leo the African (Maalouf), 201n
living abroad with children, 2–3
loneliness, 208
"look-see" visits, 13, 28

Maalouf, Amin, 201n
maps, 83
mental health, 112–120
     and schools, 113
     professionals, 114–115
middle childhood, 132–135
     and relationships, 132–134
     and school, 134

About the Author

Ngaire Jehle-Caitcheon works as a researcher, program developer, and trainer. She runs her own cross-cultural consulting company (www.caitcheon.com). Originally from New Zealand, she has spent twenty-six years abroad in North America, Australia, Europe, Africa, the Middle East, and the Mediterranean. She has been involved in intercultural training in a variety of settings, including companies, expatriate communities, and schools. She has a B.Sc. in psychology, a diploma in psychotherapy, a master's degree in sociology, and a teaching certificate for international schools. She and her husband have two children and have faced many of the situations that can arise abroad, from dealing with learning problems to preparing for evacuations during wars and rebellions.